ABOUT THE BOOK

After suffering years of anxiety and abuse, Jenny Wren-Patrick was diagnosed with bipolar disorder. And while learning about her condition helped to explain a lot of her confusion and mood swings, her consultant psychiatrist advised her to take another step forward and start to write down her life's story.

Mending Broken Lives is the result, and for Jenny, writing it has unlocked many memories both good and bad, helping her to deal with the things she had buried deep down. She has received counseling at various times but still maintains that writing it all down has been the most help, and hopefully it will help others too—whether you are another soul with bipolar disorder, a professional studying bipolar disorder, or someone who has a friend or relative with this disorder.

With the right support and understanding, there is light at the end of this long black tunnel.

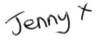

MENDING
Broken Lives

ONE WOMAN'S JOURNEY
WITH BIPOLAR DISORDER

JENNY WREN-PATRICK

authorHOUSE®

AuthorHouse™ UK
1663 Liberty Drive
Bloomington, IN 47403 USA
www.authorhouse.co.uk
Phone: 0800 047 8203 (Domestic TFN)
+44 1908 723714 (International)

Published by AuthorHouse 08/27/2019

ISBN: 978-1-7283-9208-0 (sc)
ISBN: 978-1-7283-9221-9 (hc)
ISBN: 978-1-7283-9209-7 (e)

Print information available on the last page.

All names have been changed.

This book is printed on acid-free paper.

CONTENTS

PREFACE

This book is intended to help both of us—you and me.

Perhaps you are another soul with bipolar disorder. It may be that you know someone else with this diagnosis and want to try to understand. Even if you are a professional who is trying to understand what it's like to have bipolar disorder, I hope this book goes some way to help you to understand too. I am learning to live with bipolar disorder, trying to uncover some of the causes of this miserable condition, to understand which stresses may trigger it in a person already predisposed to it, and to cope with having it as well as I can.

Having had a troubled early life of my own, which was then compounded by the serious life-threatening illness of my new husband and then further disrupted by my giving birth to a complex child with severe autistic tendencies, and subsequently receiving my own diagnosis of bipolar disorder, I am pleased to be able to say that I am at last settled, content with life, and have enjoyed an amazing career working with children who have special educational needs. I feel that I have been able to give back all the help I received, both in my own life and that of my son.

If you had ever asked me as a child how I thought things would turn out for me, I would not have believed it was possible to feel like I do now as a normal, well-adjusted adult, but nevertheless—here I am!

CHAPTER 1

GROWING UP

I was born in Bristol, although our home at the time was in the town of Locking, which is near Weston-super-Mare, thirty miles from Bristol. My birth was induced early in case I had a different blood type from my mum, as her blood group (D rhesus negative) was of a very rare type. Her doctors were worried that I may have needed a blood transfusion at birth; I didn't, luckily. I was born three weeks before I was due and was tiny, weighing only five pounds. My dad was in the Royal Air Force (RAF), so we were regularly moved on and posted to live and work all over the world. My brother, Jeremy, two and a half years older than me, was born abroad whilst my parents were stationed there.

Three weeks after I was born, we were moved on from our home in RAF Locking to live in RAF Stoke Hammond. We lived there until I was eighteen months old. Jeremy started school there. When we left, bound for the RAF base at Changi, Singapore, Jeremy's teacher asked Mum to keep in touch with his class, so she did. She sent them long, interesting letters about our journey and our new lives there. The teacher typed them out in full (as Mum's handwriting was very hard to read) when she received them and turned them into a scrapbook, complete with all the photographs Mum sent with them and letters written by Jeremy himself. She used the letters and photographs productively in her geography lessons. She presented Mum with the book when we returned to England two years later. The scrapbook, titled *Jeremy's Journey*, is a fascinating journal of our years living in Singapore which one day I would like to see in print.

My earliest memories are of living in Singapore, dancing on our morning walk with the monkeys running along beside us and in the trees on our way to school for Jeremy and kindergarten for me. I remember the huge mosquitoes hanging in the air around us; Nancy, our *amah* (mum's helper); and Cocky, our neighbour's white cockatoo with a yellow crest. Cocky didn't really belong to them. The previous tenants left him behind in the married quarters, where my friend Jonathon and his family lived. Cocky could imitate Jonathon so well that his mother often mistakenly thought that Jonathon had called her, which my mum found very funny!

Uniforms in the kindergarten and infants' school were pink-and-white check dresses for the girls; they had to wear blue-and-white dresses in the junior section. The boys all wore white shorts and smart white short-sleeved shirts with a picture of a palm tree on the pocket. Mum told me later that the palm tree symbol was the old gallows used to hang people!

While we had our Singaporean amah, the family next door had a Malay girl who helped their mum look after Jonathon and his two older sisters. Betty, Jonathon's elder sister, was nine, and Serena was seven. Their mum had to leave the family in the care of her Malay girl to go home to England, as her mother had died. While she was away, my mum asked if there was anything she could do to help them. Mum was brilliant at making clothes for Jeremy and me, and for Dad and herself too. The Malay girl was very pleased and asked Mum to make some blue-and-white checked school dresses for Serena, as she was changing schools and entering the junior section. Mum did so happily, but she was surprised their mum had gone back to England without first preparing Serena for junior school.

Just after we arrived in Singapore, I had a nasty accident at the swimming pool. I was in the very shallow safety pool for little children, and luckily right in front of my mum. Apparently I yelled, "Look, Mum," as I jumped in backwards! I hit my face on the pool's side as I went into the water. Mum fished me out immediately, but not before I had lost my two front teeth. There was a lot of blood, and no one could find my teeth;

they were completely gone. The dentist on the RAF base said I must have knocked them clean out. But a year later, they reappeared. I had simply knocked them straight back up into my jaw. Later, as a teenager, when my milk teeth had fallen out naturally and been replaced with adult teeth, one of them became very discoloured. An X-ray showed that the root wasn't there. The dentist I was taken to told me I must have damaged the root of the adult tooth when I fell, and that root had since been absorbed. He said it was a wonder that tooth hadn't already fallen out! I had to have it removed and replaced with a bridge when I was twenty-one years old.

My brother and I used to fight a lot even then, but he was always there for me if I needed him. Jonathon often hit me. One day I was about to hit him back with a half-brick I'd picked up when Jeremy saw us. He came over to me and said, "Here, give me that brick!" I did, rather sullenly, because I thought Jonathon needed to be taught a lesson. I was pleased when Jeremy carried on with "I can hit him harder than you can!"

I must have been only three or four in those memories, as I was four when we came home to England. I remember the flight; it was in an RAF VC10. And I remember having to wear sunglasses so that I could look out the window. I was told never to look straight at the sun, but I did. I took very fast, darting glimpses, which burned a satisfying hole in my vision—a brief sight of a pure white circle, followed by a tiny black circle imposed on everything I looked at for a while. I know now I literally burnt a patch on my retina, but at the time it was just an experiment with my life; I was a naughty little girl who always looked so sweet but had a determination for having her own way. It belied my tiny stature to my advantage.

I have happy memories of always being allowed to crawl onto the nearest lap for a snooze wherever I was and being cocooned in my mother's arms, listening to her chatting with her friends. I recall her steady heartbeat and breathing; the comforting voice of her conversations; the ums, yeses, and nos with the little nod of her head, which rocked me to sleep against her chest; and the ready laughter which ensured a steady supply of willing listeners and friends to talk to during many an afternoon nap. I often sat on my teacher's lap at kindergarten too. At the end of the school day, at story time, I would be tucked up on her warm lap, listening to the story whilst she thought I was asleep. Everyone else sat cross-legged at her feet, mouths open, drinking in the stories. The stories were longer than they should have been so as not to wake me up!

My teacher protested at my having to go to school. "But she's so small," she told my mum. And I was, apparently measuring just thirteen inches from my collar to the hem of my home-made school dress and over-pants made to match. One of my earliest school photos shows me standing angelically, determined not to get too close to the boy next to me. My teacher was directly behind me, looking down at me and smiling. Happy days!

When we arrived home in England, I think I remember the taxi ride from the airport. We passed some cows in a field, much to our amazement. And to the driver's amusement, we hopped up and down, excitedly looking at these huge black-and-white beasts. We'd never seen cows before. But, of course, to us, monkeys were commonplace. I say I "think" I remember, as I have heard the story so often before I don't know if it's the story of it or the actual incident that I'm remembering.

The rest of my early childhood passed reasonably happily. We continued to move every two years or so, never really putting down many deep roots and leaving behind half-remembered best friends, houses, schools, Sunday school lessons in one village with Auntie Molly at church, and various pets.

Unfortunately, at the same time, I had an increasing feeling that all was not right with my dad. He gradually changed from being a happy-go-lucky, cheerful daddy who came home whistling each evening in his boiler suit or flying overalls with the Velcro fastenings—which we pulled open as fast as he could close them again, laughing—to a morose, unpredictable man who was, more often than not, drunk. He beat my brother and me into the middle of next week at the slightest misdemeanour, and I became afraid of him.

In the summer of 1973, we lived near Chelmsford. I was seven, and my brother was ten. Our best friends were the Somersets, Paul and Angela; we did everything together, attending school and enjoying a carefree childhood. Mum used to make us fish and chips in newspaper when we played in our den at the bottom of the garden. And I remember we sometimes went to the fair together, with our pocket money.

Jeremy was behaving rather badly and was too interested in Angela (and me, too, for that matter). He insisted on looking at our genitals whenever we were alone with him. But Angela and I thought it was just normal kid stuff and didn't complain to anyone about it, although we didn't like it.

I remember that year I bought my first ever record—a single by the Carpenters titled "Please Mr Postman". Memories of that house include eating in our dining room and that we sometimes ate crisps called Discos whilst watching TV after school, if Dad wasn't there.

We owned our first dog here, a black mongrel called Judy. Dad insisted she was kept outside and she often ran away, so he had her tethered up, and one day mum said she had found her over the fence dangling by the tether, almost hanged, so she made the tether longer, and we begged to be allowed to keep her in the house instead, but to no avail.

Dad was becoming very unpredictable; he was often drunk and usually very angry, and one day he met us on our way home from school, rolling drunk, and he told us that he had had Judy put to sleep, as he thought it was for the best. We were inconsolable, and Mum was very angry with Dad, not to mention the vet, for doing that to a perfectly good dog.

Mum secretly told us later, as a sort of explanation, that Dad had become an alcoholic and wasn't aware of how unreasonably he was behaving at the moment. I had noticed he was certainly spending most of his time either staying very late at work or in the pub down the road. I was happy that I didn't see much of him actually! But I was furious with him over the loss of my beautiful black dog, and what little respect I may have had left, as far as he was concerned, was lost forever that very day.

When he was at home with us, he was always extremely short-tempered, and he didn't want to have to hear Jeremy or me talking at all without his permission, even to the point of insisting that if Jeremy or I wanted to speak, then we had to put our hands up like we did at school. Once, to my horror, when Jeremy entered the dining room and casually spoke to Mum, Dad, sitting at the table, lashed out so hard and fast that Jeremy was hit and smashed against the wall behind him, and Dad was livid with him for making him jump! I learned from Jeremy one day much later on that Dad had once actually killed a man in the same fashion; the man had jumped out from behind him and attempted to mug Dad, and Dad had karate-chopped his neck and killed him. I wasn't sure whether to believe him or not.

Dad sometimes had visitors. I later learned that they were some sort of counsellors. I remember very daringly entering the living room once when a visitor was there talking with Dad (we were *not* allowed to go in the living room if Dad was in there), marching in, and putting up my hand to speak. Dad went a funny shade of purple, but I knew I was quite safe if he had a guest. He ignored me, and I stood there for ages, with his visitor growing ever more embarrassed.

Eventually Dad threw his chair backwards with a howl of rage, stood up, grabbed me, and took me through to the kitchen, where he upended me and spanked me repeatedly so hard on the bottom that I blanked it out and honestly didn't feel a thing. I was so high with the success I had had at annoying him for a change that I really couldn't have cared less; I was just hoping to embarrass him, and it seemed I had been successful. Dad then went back to the living room as if nothing at all had happened. Later, when his visitor had left, I felt slightly afraid of what Dad would do to me, so I sat at the top of the stairs, ready to run and hide if he came for me. I was delighted with my bonus reward when I heard his plaintive voice wobbling and calling to Mum, saying, "I hurt my hand ..." I said to myself, "*Yes!* Serves him right!"

Mum did try to explain to us around that time that Dad was ill. She said that he had even been a resident at a mental hospital called Honey Lane for quite a long while, and it was true that we had visited him there once or twice without realising what it was. Jeremy and I, bored at having nothing to do during one visit, went to look around the grounds, and we were fascinated to come across an open window outside of which there was a huge pile of used hypodermic needles and syringes. We didn't get to go to visit again!

One day Mum said that she was now making her own supply of home-brewed ale for Dad (which we had noticed, as the bottles kept exploding in the cubby hole beneath the stairs), because if she didn't, then he would drink at the pub, and then she would have absolutely no control over how much he was drinking. We both thought that she was quite mad as it was obvious that she wanted him to stop drinking but here she was making the stuff herself for him, but this new reasoning made more sense.

She said that dad had serious digestive difficulties and that he had had to have a lot of his stomach removed because of ulcers (which was why he was in hospital for so long, we had thought) and that his doctor had recommended he drink at least one pint of beer a day to help his digestion, but that Dad had now started drinking more than that and had become dependent on the alcohol. He was unable to digest a lot of food and was living on a very bland diet including white tripe cooked in milk, and steamed fish, which we thought was disgusting. I didn't really understand the implications of all this information at the time, though I did begin to realise that he couldn't help being like he was. I still hated him though, and I couldn't help that either.

Jeremy and his friends often stole strawberries that summer from the local allotments by the park, and once, when I was dragged along too, we were caught, and I was grabbed by the allotment owner along with Jeremy, and we were told to tell him where we lived. I blurted out our real address. Jeremy was absolutely livid with me. Of course, he had lied about that too, and because I had told the truth, he knew that the allotment owner would go to our house, and he thought Dad would "kill" us, so he made me run away from home with him. We didn't get far, and when we went back home later, no one had noticed anyway! I told Mum because I was so scared the police would come, and I can never lie anyway. We were soundly told off, but nothing much came of it.

Jeremy and his friends were being quite nasty to me at the time; they would take me along with them going crayfish spotting, and they would find lots of them in the stream that was near to our school. I was fascinated, having always loved wildlife of any type, but on one occasion Jeremy decided to be especially vindictive and mean to me, as he knew how much it would upset me. He took all of the crayfish that he had caught up on to the bridge that went over the stream, and he started dropping the crayfish into the water from quite a height, saying, "This one can go free … This one can go free …", until he got to the last one, which he dismembered limb by limb, dropping each bit into the water whilst I cried and begged him to stop, but to no avail.

On another occasion, Jeremy and I were given some pocket money because the mop fair was in the village, and so we went with Paul and Angela, our friends who lived near to us. Jeremy won a goldfish on one of the stalls, and I was thrilled to have a new pet, so he gave it to me and won another for himself. On the way home, he suddenly grabbed my fish bag and tied them both together and hung them over a low branch by the path. He laughingly told me that he was going to put pin holes in the bags and watch them die. I was so upset. He produced a safety pin from his pocket and said I could save one of the fish if I pricked the other bag myself. I did nothing of the sort but ran home crying because I couldn't bear to watch his cruelty, but really the cruelty was directed at me.

Dad had changed jobs while we lived here; he was no longer in the Royal Air Force, and he now worked for Marconi as a technical author. It was a good thing, really, since while we were living here we suddenly learned that we had to go and live with my granny in Royal Leamington Spa, in Warwickshire. She was very old, unwell and—worse, from my point of view—not at all fond of her only granddaughter.

CHAPTER 2

OUR MOVE TO THE MIDLANDS

We had a nightmare journey of over one hundred miles in a hired white van. Jeremy and I slid around on the settee cushions in the back with no seat belts or proper seats or anything like that. At the end of it, as we pulled into the U-shaped drive of my granny's house, an ambulance pulled out of it on the other side. Granny had fallen and broken her hip and was going to hospital.

Living in her house with her was horrible. It was a huge Victorian house with absolutely no heating installed, so it was cold and damp. Granny's dog, Tats, would mess in her room rather than go outside into the garden, so behind her settee were mounds of dog poo, and her room stank. Tats was also infested with fleas, so our dog also caught them (we had a cairn terrier called Pip), and both dogs spent all day underneath Granny's bed, which was also in her room, scratching themselves raw on the springs underneath it. In the evenings, Mum and I would sit with a bowl of water each and catch the fleas by hand and then drown them in the water. We would catch at least thirty each, every night, and it became a game—a horrible one—stopping them from floating and escaping. I was also covered with flea bites and scratched all the time.

Our sitting room was the old dining room at the back of the house. My bedroom was the box room on the second floor along with the bathroom, in the middle of the two-part staircase. I hated being right behind the bathroom, especially when the flush was pulled, as it made a tremendous noise. Mum had made my bedroom nice, though, with a navy-blue velvet curtain around my clothes rail, and pretty blue wallpaper.

At some point I changed bedrooms, moving into Jeremy's old room above the front door. This room was quite a bit bigger than my old one, and Jeremy moved into a double bedroom next door.

I was not safe from Jeremy in this new room; it was right next to his, and he would come in and grab me by my arm and march me into his room whenever he felt like it. His exploration of my genitals became a daily occurrence, whenever Mum and Dad were out or busy.

Mum and Dad had the other double bedroom at the back. Our kitchen was large, and we had to go down a small flight of scullery steps to get to it, and the cellar door was behind the kitchen door. The cellar was dark and damp, and we didn't use it, but it was a scary place to be if we did go down for any reason!

Mum had a home help here who was employed to help with the cleaning and care of the house so Mum could care for Granny. Joan was lovely, but even she couldn't get me out of bed in the mornings. She took to making my breakfast for me so that the smells of bacon and egg, or her special breakfast pizza, would waft upstairs and tempt me out. She taught me how to cook it too, which was fun. She wasn't supposed to cook for us, but she was so helpful and tried anything to help Mum deal with us children too.

Granny was very deaf, so her TV was on maximum loudness all the time, and so we all had to listen when Emmerdale Farm came on each evening. She was also an alcoholic, seemingly living on sherry, which she drank like water. Mum tried to dilute it once, but then she found that Granny just drank twice as much. Once Granny even drank some vegetable oil thinking it was sherry, and that didn't do her much good. She had a commode in her room (to add to the smell in there) which Mum had to empty.

Granny always wanted company, and I was the only one who would ever give up any time for her. We played cards together almost every evening, but she was still horrible to me, tickling and scratching me whenever she could catch me and complaining loudly that I wasn't doing enough for her. My mum's sister, my aunty Nan, and her family came each Sunday for lunch, and then we all played cards afterwards, which I always enjoyed immensely. Aunty Nan lived only a short way away from Granny, but as she was a busy architect with a husband and a family of two boys, she said she couldn't possibly give up her life to look after her mother, so it fell to my mum as the only other daughter to give up her life instead, which annoyed her considerably. Mum gave up everything to look after her own mum, and her only escape was to go to Women's Institute meetings, which she did every other Thursday.

My brother and I were then taken up with the business of starting at yet another school. He was going to his new secondary school, and I was off to my new primary school, which didn't seem to have a uniform as far as I remember; photos from there are of me in home clothes. We each went to at least five different schools before we settled into our secondary schools, so we were both very behind in lots of subjects. Jeremy went to school on our very first day in Leamington Spa, but he got sent home immediately, as he was in the wrong blazer, and so Mum took off the red edging for him and sent him straight back, very cross with the school. She said she had had no choice about which school he went to, so the school should have had no choices either. He was known thereafter as the boy who had the wrong uniform, which must have been difficult for him.

My mum must also have had a hard time of it, caring for her unhappy alcoholic husband; her alcoholic mother, who was elderly and slipping into dementia; *and* two difficult children. My brother, being twelve or thirteen at that time and uprooted from friends, was a typical rebellious teenager. I bore the brunt of his sexual abuse and was displaying strange facial tics and knee jerks. I was finding school increasingly frustrating.

Our one happiness was our dogs. Pip's first litter gave us a lovely female to keep, whom we called Jip, but she died when she contracted parvovirus as a very young pup, which was horribly upsetting for all of us. Pip was a good brood bitch, though, and we had lots more litters of puppies to sell. We kept another one of our female puppies; we called her Gypsy (Gyp), and she also proved to be a good mother, so we often had lots of puppies around, which Jeremy and I loved. If either Pip or Gyp had puppies anytime, then the other one would also begin to lactate and feed the puppies, so the pups always had two mothers with milk, and they grew very well.

I was bullied from the start at my school by a girl called Lesley and her gang, and I had only one good friend there. My friend was from another RAF family, and she lived quite locally, so we walked to school and back together each day with her little brother. Her dad was an officer in the RAF, so her parents looked down on us as being just a sergeant's family, but we didn't care. We went to Guides together each week too once we were ten and played together every day after school either at our house or theirs. Jeremy was a pain with her though since he obviously liked her and pestered us, never leaving us alone if Mum was out, leaving us with him to do as he liked. It was awful, and we didn't know how to stop him.

There were other children living near to us, and I made friends with a girl called Terrie and her brother Hugh, who also lived in our road. There was also a boy called Mario Coke who sometimes liked to play with us in the alleyway behind our houses. Mario's family were Italian, and he had a very strong Italian accent. He had a mop of black hair, and he was a bit strange to say the least; Terrie and I never played with him alone; we played with him only if all of us were there together. He lived in the only "modern" house in his road, and my mum said that it was odd that a foreign family should live there now, as during the war it had been owned by a man who flouted the blackout rules regularly and it had subsequently been the only house hit by a bomb on the night of the Coventry Blitz. It had received a direct hit and had to be rebuilt.

I clearly remember one day when we had all been playing together before tea; Terrie had been called in for hers, and I was going in for mine. Mario suddenly roughly grabbed me and told me that I had to come out again after tea, as he wanted to carry on the game. I assumed that Terrie would come out again too, so I went out to meet them, but before I did, I had a strange feeling about it, and I went up to my room to change clothes. I put on a pair of shorts, a pair of tracksuit bottoms, a T-shirt, a pair of denim dungarees, a sweatshirt, and a jumper. I must have looked like the Michelin tyre man!

Anyway, as soon as I opened our back gate, Mario was there, and he grabbed me again and forced me behind a large white van that was parked there. He tried to get my clothes off, but I went as limp as a rag doll as he tried to remove the layers; he got so frustrated that he threw me down and ran off. I calmly went back indoors, changed again, and stayed in the house for the evening. I never told a soul, and indeed I had forgotten all about it until I started writing this all down!

A few years later, after I was married, I heard about an incident that had happened near our old house. A young girl had seen a young man with a shock of black hair indecently exposing himself to her. I immediately wondered if it might have been Mario. I was sure I had seen him around still. In fact, I was certain that it was him once when I met a postman delivering around that area one day; he looked just the same as Mario had when we were children.

It was after I caught myself doing more strange things that my situation changed. I was prone to often make backward jerks of my legs to kick myself whenever I walked anywhere and to bend my arms sharply at the elbow to crash my arm muscles together, and, to my shame, I even made the *V* sign at people when they weren't looking. I made it to my teacher, Mr Robinson, one day, to my horror—I couldn't stop myself. He saw me, and I was caught and told off soundly, and he was very upset. He was my absolute favourite teacher, and I had offended him totally.

When walking I also found that I just *had* to go around lampposts, and then if I tried to carry on walking, I just had to go back and "unwind" myself before I could go on. It took me ages to get anywhere! People began to give me strange looks, and I hated it but couldn't stop. I was also still making strange noises—guttural tics, outbursts that I couldn't help—and the knee jerks were getting worse. I developed a tummy ache to try to get out of going to school and became miserable at home. I was unable to get up in the mornings and disliked school.

Soon I was attracting even more attention from teachers, as I couldn't concentrate; I was always spoiling my work and not managing homework.

I would do some writing and then suddenly scribble all over it in a frenzy or find myself spitting on it.

My mum bought the school photo that year, and she was aghast at the change in me. The previous photo was of a confident normal youngster—albeit with a swollen lower lip due to falling out of bed one night—but the new one was of a very pale, strained young girl who looked utterly miserable.

Mum took the photos to my doctor to see what he thought, and he was worried too. She also took them to the head of my school to ask his opinion, and together they decided that I needed to be out of the home situation, and a boarding school was discussed. I was asked if I would like to go to see a school nearby—a boarding school. At the interview, I was shown around a lovely looking establishment with houses of about ten or twelve girls in each, with dormitories of four girls in each, a huge community room with massive scatter cushions to loll on, house parents for each house, small classrooms for school, and friendly staff.

Would I like to go? Would I like to leave my horrible Granny, with her chain-smoking, her foul dog-poo-ridden room, and her long, yellow-stained fingernails which were always either digging into me or tickling me? Would I like to leave my brother, who was turning into someone I really didn't want to know? Would I like to leave my mother, who was so busy I hardly ever had any time with her? Would I like to leave the school where I was bullied and miserable, and had earned the nickname Horse-face? You bet!

I had my long plaits cut off because I said I wanted to look like a boy. Mum only agreed because I was going off to boarding school and wouldn't be able to manage my long hair. I prepared delightedly for what I hoped was going to be a wonderful time for me.

Our last litter of pups was the one that I managed to have an accident with; holding a puppy and running down the garden path one day, I tripped and went sprawling. I, putting the pup first as usual, kept the puppy safe but didn't save myself. I hurt my abdomen, and it was so painful I ended up going to hospital at midnight with a burst appendix.

CHAPTER 3

BOARDING SCHOOL

It was the year I was twelve when I had a spell in hospital with appendicitis and subsequent peritonitis. I spent a month in hospital during the summer holidays of 1977. I was rushed to hospital in the night and operated on immediately. When I awoke, I had a board strapped to my arm and a drip was going into my arm. I was very unwell for a long time. When I finally had my stitches removed, the doctor did a double-take when he saw me; he was surprised that I had even survived. Mine had been the worst case he had ever seen, and he said he had had to remove all my intestines to try to sort out the many abscesses that were strewn around my abdomen. He had sprinkled my intestines with antibiotic powder and tumbled them all back in, not really expecting me to survive the night. When I was fully recovered, I left home to go and live at the boarding school in Kenilworth. It was supposed to save me from the tensions at home and get me back on track with my schoolwork, but it didn't pan out like that.

The school was filled with other girls who all had problems of their own at home and school, and it seemed to me that we were all lumped together for want of somewhere else we could go. During my first week, I was ushered into the head's office. He was a very odd man—a chain smoker with yellow fingertips and teeth and very curly grey hair. He was a northerner and sounded very much like my dad with his accent, which was either Lancashire or Yorkshire—I never found out which. He asked me if I knew why I was there at his school, which I didn't really, and he explained that the girls were all something called "maladjusted", which meant that they didn't fit in at home or at school. Well, that was me all right, and I was quite happy about it. He also said I shouldn't tell anyone else that.

I soon settled into school life there. We all had our "jobs" to do each day, which were on a rota basis, so we took turns. We either (1) washed the hand basins and shook out bedside rugs outside, (2) washed the baths out properly, (3) swept the floor in our little bit of the house, (4) swept the back stairs, or (5) swept the main stairs. We also took turns at doing the sixth job, which was being the "job checker." No one could leave until her job was done and had been checked. Nobody wore shoes or socks during the day, because at the end of each day, before supper in our common rooms, we had to wash our own "smalls" and put them to dry on the radiators in the common room, and nobody wanted to wash socks! Each week we had to produce our laundry, which the housemother listed in her laundry book. When it came back, she would tick it all off again so no one's clothes got mixed up. She would comment if there weren't many clothes for the laundry that week, making us go back and find something she knew had been worn but which we hadn't brought through. The housemothers were very strict about laundry.

We had breakfast, lunch, and dinner in the dining room all together each day; the adult on our table went and got our tray of food to share for each meal. At morning break, we always queued at the hatch for leftover toast from breakfast and cold chocolate, which was milk with drinking chocolate on top; we ate the chocolate with a teaspoon and then drank the milk. When someone had a birthday, we had a birthday tea, which was our usual cooked dinner, but pudding was "splodge", which was mousse (any flavour the birthday girl wanted—I always had butterscotch) with chocolate vermicelli on top. There was always a birthday cake too (flavour chosen by the birthday girl—I always had chocolate cake) to share with everyone. The birthday girl took the trays of cake to each table, and everyone was encouraged to make a birthday card for her, and there was then a "secret" pile of cards on her chair when she went to sit down. I was ashamed of myself one year when a birthday card arrived for me through the post in dad's handwriting and I refused to open it in case it might be embarrassing. It turned out to be rather nice! Dad was prone to turning up to see me without warning, and when he did, he was always drunk; I was so embarrassed.

The photo taken of me that year showed me wearing my Aran jumper, a garment that I *never* took off; it was like a comfort blanket for me, and that got me teased mercilessly.

We had some wooden boxes around the community area which were open on the side which faced the cushions, and the birthday committee decorated them each month with people's birthdays on little bits of card hanging in the middle of each display, which had themes like "under the sea" or "space" or whatever they liked. I joined this committee and enjoyed doing the birthday boxes.

We had two main meetings all together each day, one in the morning and another in the evening. Each morning, after jobs, we had our first meeting of the day, where everyone sat in her place in a large circle in the community room; we always sat with our houseparents. At these meetings, there was a chairman (who had to call, "Order!" at the start to open the meeting officially, go through the agenda, and then close the meeting) and a secretary (who had to keep notes on whatever was said). We discussed jobs that one had to be nominated for and seconded, and then there was a vote. I was secretary a couple of times and chairman a few times too. If a person wanted to tell the assembled meeting (that included all the staff and girls) that someone had recently hurt her or been rude to her, then the person had to put up her hand in the "any other business" (AOB) segment and bring a complaint against the other person. This was tedious and often spiteful, and it took ages, because anyone who'd seen what had happened had to then put up his or her hand to speak too. Everyone would slump in their seats and sigh if lots of hands went up during AOB, and we all hoped it wasn't going to be about us! People would sometimes pretend to have seen something to help their friend out, and others would argue the point, and it was up to the chairman to stop it going on and on, but it always did. Sometimes someone would "bring a compliment" against someone, which was much nicer!

Most of the girls seemed to me to be at the school just so they wouldn't get themselves pregnant before the age of sixteen. Some were self-harmers, and lots kept running away. The latter lived in their pyjamas; no clothes were allowed in case they got out again, and nobody in the local neighbourhood ever batted an eyelid when a pyjama-clad teenager was seen out and about and then being hauled back to the school. We were classed as social outcasts, and the neighbours generally wanted nothing to do with any of us.

Most of the other girls, I soon found, had found themselves "special friends" amongst the adults at the school. The term "special friend" was given to an adult or couple to whom an individual girl had attached herself; these adults would help and support her as proper parents would. My special friends were very new to the school too and didn't have any other special friends when I first met them. They were married, although Hayleigh had kept her own surname, and I was at first much more attracted to Dan, and he became my special friend before Hayleigh did too. Dan had strange eyes, in that one of them was blue and the other was brown with a quarter of blue in it. My brother's second daughter has eyes like that, and I think it looks rather nice! The relationship between the three of us was more like having another (non-abusive!) brother and a sister for me, and at first I found it hard to share them with other girls who latched on later, as I was their first special friend at the school, and they were mine. I learned in later years that one of my "rivals", a girl who'd had big ears and a huge complex about it, had committed suicide after having two children by two different fathers and then having a mental breakdown. That was very upsetting for me to hear about, and I wanted to put time back and share my special friends with her more, as they'd been so wonderful and supportive to me.

I lived there for the first two years happily enough, getting through the terms and going home for holidays, before I realised that no one was especially interested in teaching me. Although we did have classrooms and school time, no one really worked. My special friend Dan was an English teacher by trade, so he taught me a lot about English language and literature. Other girls weren't so lucky, but some taught themselves to type, and others learned to play guitars (I did both). I, however, knew I needed to pass my school exams if I was ever going to fulfil my dream of becoming a veterinary surgeon.

I asked about going out to the school which was next door to ours; other girls went there from the boarding school, and I began to get excited and dream of having a future that I had thought I might have lost forever. I got the distinct impression that I would be able to go to the other school for the next term. Over the next summer holidays, I was so sure I would be going there that Mum even began to buy my uniform for me. We bought second-hand items where we could. I knew the uniform colours, so we could get my shirts, jerseys, and skirts, but I still needed a school tie and the PE kit, so I phoned to ask about the uniform list during the holidays. I joyfully got through to my special friend Dan, but I was quickly told in no uncertain terms that they didn't think I was quite ready yet. I was so upset that mum took the phone from me and spoke to him herself. Dan, at school, told her he had heard the metaphorical slap I had felt!

I went back to boarding school after the holidays, absolutely determined to show them how wrong they were, and I did eventually manage to persuade everyone that I was ready.

I started going out to school after Christmas, but of course I was too late to take any options, and I had to take the exam courses that were left with any spaces. I was *so* annoyed. I missed out on a few subjects I wanted to take—especially biology—and was irritated to be doing History 16+ instead.

When I did eventually get to go out to school normally, it was great, and after a while I was even allowed to start going home at weekends too. My new best friend at school, Debbie, sometimes came to tea at my boarding school during the week, and we would play tennis on the tennis courts and chat about school and boys and things. I loved it, and she often welcomed me back to her house on Friday nights, on my way to the bus stop to go home for the weekend, and I felt so normal for the first time in years.

I thoroughly enjoyed my time at school. I was with the same form tutor throughout my time there, and I liked him a lot. I loved art, geography,

English language and literature, and home economics (where we cooked and learned about food), and even the History 16+ class I had been forced into was interesting. I also made a few nice friends, Alison and Debbie were the best ones, and I got on well with most people. I was unfortunately singled out by the school bullies as well, though, and I had a tough time trying to get them to leave me alone.

The trouble was that I was a new girl, and I was clever. I was doing well in every subject, and PJ and her cronies were jealous. I loved art the most, but unfortunately PJ and co. were in the same class. Our teacher was in the habit of setting us off in our lesson and then going next door to talk to the other art teacher and drink coffee with her, leaving us to get on with it.

One particular day, PJ and her boyfriend Jay went too far. We were using clay to make our models. I was busy fashioning my gorilla head (which was later displayed in the school foyer as the teacher liked it so much), and Jay came right up to me, egged on by PJ, cleared his throat noisily, and spat the contents of his mouth out all along his finger. He then flicked it straight into my face. There was a shocked hush throughout the class. I didn't make a single sound. I just put down my tools and walked straight out of the classroom door, not even wiping my face. Jay gasped, "She's going to get Sir!" He was surprised when I went straight past the next-door classroom and continued into the main part of the school building. I left them all behind, strode through the corridors and went into the head's office without even knocking.

When he realised what had happened, he simply told me that I could go home (back to boarding school anyway). He phoned ahead to warn staff there that I was on my way, and he swiftly dealt with Jay, PJ, and co. himself. Let's just say the next time I ever saw them was a few years later when I was out walking and saw a very pregnant PJ out with her gaggle of crying babies and a miserable-looking husband!

When I went to my friend Debbie's wedding a few years later, I spoke to her dad, and he recognised me and said, "Oh, you're that kid from the home aren't you?" I felt so humiliated, but not after Debbie later told me that her dad had been abusing her sexually and only didn't when I was there at her house. I'd been so envious of her normal home life, and she'd been so envious of my "safe" boarding school life, yet neither of us was honest with the other, and our friendship petered out after we'd left school and both got married.

One of the first lessons I had learned at my boarding school was to stop talking; as they twisted everything I said anyway, it was easier not to try. At meal times, the adults on my table would hiss "SSSShhh, Jenny, stop chattering!" because I was silent at the table. I was also asked, quite early on, whether or not I loved my mum. I instantly replied that of course I did, and there were smug smiles all round, and Hayleigh and Dan said that I had obviously been brainwashed into thinking I actually loved my mum, because if she loved me, then I wouldn't be at this school, would I? Self-doubt began to creep in.

I remember we talked about the royal family once, and when I said that I felt we *do* need to have a queen in this country, I was immediately sat on (physically) by Dan, my special friend, who then tickled me and screamed right down my ear, and made me retract that statement, as it was "obviously your mum talking through you" and I should make up my own mind … Confusing!

I didn't know whether I even still *liked* Dan after the first time that happened, as it was so out of character for him—and terrifying for me. It was as if he had been told how to deal with me by someone else, but it became a fairly regular occurrence, and I had to admit that the "making up" of our friendship that always came afterwards was always so lovely that it almost made the fights worth having. Each fight deepened our bond, and I came to almost enjoy them.

That did happen quite a lot, until after a while I was no longer sure of my own opinions on anything. I got very angry with myself a lot there as well; I seemed to be losing my marbles. For instance, I consistently forgot that on Wednesday evenings the adults had a meeting in the main community room. This was in the centre of the school, and as such, every other area led off from it. Every Wednesday, without fail, I would walk out of our common room on my way to see someone and would suddenly find myself in the centre of a group of seemingly familiar (usually friendly) adults, but all of them would have such angry faces because I'd dared to intrude into *their* meeting place. What if I'd heard something I shouldn't, heaven forbid!

I never witnessed any sexual abuse there, but lots of other sorts of abuse, sadly, were rife; I was often shouted at, pinned down, and tickled; it became a nightmare from which I had no hope of escape—at least until I could prove that I was OK going out to school and could be trusted to spend weekends at home (and, presumably, not tell any sacred secrets to outsiders) before being eventually allowed to leave when I was sixteen. I had to endure seeing my friends treated similarly too. The staff and other girls made a lovely leaving book for me that was signed and illustrated by everyone, and they told me that I was one of their few success stories (well, I suppose I hadn't become pregnant, hadn't married a down-and-out, actually passed some exams …) and asked me to be sure to come back and see the younger girls who looked up to me so. I promised, through gritted teeth, and then let them all down because I didn't set foot there again for a very long time.

When I did go back again, about two years later, it was because I had a steady boyfriend (Nigel, who was later my husband) and was moving away, to West Sussex, to work at a boarding kennels, and I felt I was closing that chapter in my life. I was rapturously received by the adults I remembered, but all the girls I'd known had left by then. Even so, I could still smell the misery of the current "inmates", and I never went back again. I didn't work in West Sussex for long, but when I came back and went to see the old place much later, I found that it was no more.

The school had closed, the buildings had all been knocked down, and a new estate had been built over it. The school I had endured was no longer there; it was evidently considered unsuitable and had been closed for good. With hindsight, it was *never* suitable, and I feel very angry at having spent four years of my young life encased there. Even so, I have kept tenuously in touch with some of the adults I trusted, along with my special friends. One became the manager of a local support group for parents and children with disabilities, DISCS, as I discovered when my own son turned out to be autistic and I contacted them for help. It was very odd talking to him as an equal adult; he even seemed to be physically smaller than I remembered. I also kept up with my own special friends, and so I was devastated one Christmas years later when, in reply to my usual Christmas card, I learned that they had divorced and that Dan had had a subsequent mental breakdown. I still keep in touch with him; he has since remarried and divorced a second time and moved away from the midlands to Dartmoor and seems reasonably happy again. He and I play Scrabble on the Internet, and he nearly always trounces me!

The relationship I have with people from boarding school is a bit rocky, but I am determined not to break the link; it made me who I am, and I can't change that. Recently I joined Facebook on the Internet and got back in touch with lots of the girls I still remember from those days.

Though I have always said I had hated the school and my years there, in retrospect it wasn't all bad, and I did manage to stop the tics and jerks whilst there. My mum kept in touch with me a lot after the first term (no contact with home was permitted for the first term) and would then write to me each week and would phone me at prearranged times, and when the phone would start ringing after dinner when we were in our second meeting of the day, the others would hope it was for them so they could escape the meeting!

One of the better things about being at boarding school was the music group we formed. We learned to play steel drums, tin whistles, and guitars and often played folk music together, taught by two of the teachers. We even had "folk weekends" away in a caravan. It was very special, and I learned lots of lovely songs, one of which I have recorded a little of the lyric here, as it is so meaningful to me. I play it on my guitar sometimes even now.

Still He Sings

After night, there comes the day, and so the dawn shall pass away,
Through the dawn, a wondrous thing is born, comes the day.
When the Minstrel sings his song, and the people wander on,
Still, he sings, for the pleasure music brings, still he sings.

CHAPTER 4

BOYS

I was never very interested in boys, being quite a tomboy as I was, but nevertheless I usually found that there were one or two that I did like, and they often liked me too. When we lived near Chelmsford, my brother's best friend was called Paul Somerset. He had a sister who was my age. The boys would have been about ten, and Angela and I must have been about seven, and when Paul came to play, often his sister Angela did too. Soon the four of us were firm friends, and we stayed so for many years, even after we moved away.

Jeremy also liked Angela, and it was the start of many years of having to put up with his over enthusiastic interest in and (sexual) abuse of my friends and me, which became very frustrating! It seemed normal at the time though, and it carried on throughout our childhoods, so I didn't feel too badly about it with Angela being the object as well at the time.

Paul, her brother, was very special to me, and even after we moved away up to the midlands, as soon as he was old enough to get a motorbike, he would come to see us whenever he could, and Jeremy would go to see him on his motorbike too, as they were still close friends. When I was about sixteen and he was probably about eighteen, Paul was killed in an accident when he hit a patch of oil on the road and his motorbike hit a lamppost. He was put onto a life support machine but didn't recover, and he died, leaving his organs to many other people. Angela told Jeremy, when he went down for Paul's funeral, that Paul had been getting very interested in me (the feeling had been mutual then), but we never told each other how we had been feeling. I couldn't go to the funeral, as it was held on a weekday and I was still at school. And anyway, no one knew how I felt about Paul, and I wasn't invited. I am not sure if I would have coped well anyway, as Jeremy said lots of girls came to the funeral; it seems Paul was very well liked by other girls too.

While I belonged to the Venture Scout unit at our church when I was sixteen, there was a boy there called Dave who liked me, but I liked his best friend Andrew instead. He and I were very good friends but nothing more. Dave was very persistent, but I only really thought of him as a friend. In hindsight, it was obvious that he felt rather differently; he followed me everywhere. Even when I left home to go and live with my friend Ann with her dogs, he would turn up on his bicycle and help me to walk them before cycling home ten miles again. He even gate-crashed my hen night in October 1985, crying, to tell me he had thought I was going to wait for him. I felt awful! I really had no idea he felt so strongly. He emigrated to New Zealand soon after I was married, but he did come back and visit me when he heard on the grapevine that I had had Charles. He turned up on the doorstep and sullenly said he thought he should come and see the "little rug rat", which was more than a bit creepy. I felt as though I had ruined his life and felt very guilty about it for years. We had mutual friends who sometimes told me how he was getting on, and it was never good news; he was sleeping around, taking part in dangerous sports, and even smoking, drinking, and taking drugs. He had always been a daredevil when it came to rock-climbing and sports like that, but he was incredibly fit and healthy, quite the health food and healthy lifestyle freak, and I knew that he was now no longer respecting himself and was living recklessly. It's hard to enjoy yourself when you feel so guilty about how you have treated someone else, but I swear I never meant to hurt him.

While I was still enjoying having Dave just as a friend (and nothing more), there was someone else I was attracted to who was a friend of a friend. He was called Seth, and he was twenty-four. Seth and I went out together for over a year until his sexual demands became too much to bear.

I did give in once to try to get him to change the record, but of course it only made him worse, and I hated myself for giving in, so I broke it off with him when I went to live with Ann and her dogs. I didn't even tell him where I'd gone. Dave remained a friend, but he was pleased when I broke it off with Seth.

I was really fed up with boys (including my brother) pestering me for sexual favours by then. Dave never once did, but Jeremy was really taking things too far by this time; by the time I was fourteen or fifteen, he had progressed to wanting oral sex from me, which I resisted, but he still wanted to have a close look at my genitals regularly and one day was caught by Mum walking in on him doing so. She was very angry with him, and I was so relieved, thinking that she must stop him. I felt thankful that she would deal with him while I was away and that it would stop, but she appeared to have been wearing blinkers, and nothing ever came of that.

He even tried to break my hymen one day soon after that with his finger; he had said he just wanted to feel it and promised to stop when I said so, but when I told him to stop because he was hurting me too much, he jabbed upwards hard to try to break it. I was crying out in pain, but he didn't care. Mum never spoke about it again, and I really think maybe she thought that if she ignored it, it would go away. That would have been nice.

While we were both going to Venture Scouts regularly at a local church, Jeremy tried to convince me that what we were doing was perfectly normal and that every brother did this to his sister. He said that he thought all our friends at Ventures were doing just the same. He actually said he was doing me a favour so that when I had a real boyfriend, he would think I was "a natural", and that being brilliant at sex would be something I would be pleased about!

Honestly, I wish I'd just thumped him now, or told Dave so he could have done so for me. But of course, everything is easier with hindsight.

I met Nigel through Venture Scouts. He and Jeremy had been scouts together for a long time actually, but I hadn't really noticed Nigel then, and Jeremy did not like him, referring to him as "that wimp", although he did like Samuel, Nigel's younger brother. When I was seventeen and chairman of the Venture unit, I organised a barbeque for the Ventures and invited all members who had recently left, including Nigel, who was twenty-three. He replied saying he couldn't come as he was going to be away at sea (he was a sailor), but then he turned up at a Venture meeting a few weeks later asking to talk to me. He said he could come after all. I was quite smitten with him, but I thought he was probably too old for me after the mistakes I'd made with Seth. Nigel did come to the barbeque, and I just stood and watched him; he was gorgeous! He was so sociable, talking easily with everyone, and I really began to like him.

CHAPTER 5

AFTER SCHOOL

Having survived a stormy school life, at age sixteen I was ready to really enjoy being free from everything that had been holding me back. I had finished my exams at school and was pleased with the results, considering. I got a certificate of school education (CSE) grade one in English literature, and a grade two in both English language and geography. I had got away at last from boarding school, and I was now employed full-time at the veterinary surgery at the top of the town. I had started working there on Thursday evenings after school, having had permission to go home on the bus after school on Thursdays and go back to boarding school on Fridays for a year to "keep my foot in the door".

I would have loved to have become a vet myself, but I was happy being the general dogsbody; I now looked after the cat boarding house, cleaned the hospital kennels each day, and assisted at surgeries. I was also learning to drive on my afternoon off each week and studying at college three nights a week to gain three more O levels.

The CSE grade one I had gained at school was equivalent to an O-level grade C, which was a pass, and so I studied English language and geography to boost them up to O-level grade C as well. I also studied human biology for the first time and was delighted to get grade B in that subject after only one year of studying it. I knew that I had to have at least four O-levels at a C grade or above to start training to be an animal nursing auxiliary, which was better than nothing. The vets' practice where I worked was a training facility, and I thought that I only had to get the required exams and await my turn to start at the bottom. It was a very busy year for me, but once I'd passed all three extra O-levels and my driving test, I excitedly asked to see the senior vet at the practice to discuss my future. I was devastated when his only advice for me, having congratulated me on my exam successes, was to look around elsewhere at other veterinary surgeries, or perhaps try to get a position as a dog walker with the Guide Dogs centre in the town.

He explained that, as I knew, he had just lost his head nurse, who had moved away. I was hoping to be starting at the bottom of the ladder, but he pulled the ladder rungs away from me and employed another head nurse instead of moving everybody up one rung of the ladder as we all expected him to do. We were all very upset, especially as the new head nurse was not at all friendly and managed to upset everyone very quickly. I hid my disappointment and carried on working as usual, but without the enthusiasm I'd had before. Now I was looking not at a career but at a dead-end job which was very hard work, and so I was pleasantly surprised when one of the more elderly customers singled me out and asked if I would like to help her with her large family of Boston terriers, whom she bred for show and showed all over the country.

I had met the eccentric Mrs B. when she'd brought her little bitch Trilby in to be mated. I had supervised the mating personally, as all the vets felt it was a waste of time, as generally the mating between these smart little dogs rarely results in pregnancy. I had kept an eye on the two dogs, and when they seemed ready, I had encouraged them and made sure they were not disturbed, and the result was a very healthy litter!

I worked with Mrs B. for over a year, still working full-time at the vets' but also looking after the dogs at her home when she was away and going with her to shows at weekends, including Crufts. I also stayed with her at her other house in Anglesey, where she had a smallholding with a small herd of rare breed sheep, including Jacobs and Manx Loughton sheep, and also a miniature Dexter bull, whenever I took annual leave. The vets all laughed at me about our friendship, but I had a wonderful time, and I got lots of experience showing dogs for her, even taking third at Crufts one year, which I was very proud of. I was very sorry when she died, but I was soon asked by another customer at the vets' if I would like to help her. This was my chance to escape from Seth, so I grabbed it with both hands!

Ann was a psychiatric nurse. She also owned seven basset hounds and needed help with them, as she was going back to full-time work shortly at Hatton Hospital near Warwick. Her husband, David, was working as a psychiatric nurse too, but he worked in Riyadh, in Saudi Arabia, and came home only occasionally. I moved in and became her full-time dog carer and had a wonderful time with all the dogs; they were such fun. The bassets were Dylan and Benson, the parents of the litter (Dylan was a lemon basset, while Benson was the more usual black and tan); Sam, Dylan's sister, another lemon; and their pups, all black and tan: Fred (of course!), Hedges (to go with Benson), Pluto, and Grunty (my favourite). The next time David arrived home for a holiday, Ann got pregnant, and so after nine months, when Ann had to go back to work, I was looking after seven dogs *and* her baby, a girl called Katie. It was very hard work but great fun. I sorted out her vegetable patch and planted all her vegetables for her whenever Katie had a nap, and I walked the dogs in the evenings when Ann got home.

I was both amazed and delighted when Nigel became my next boyfriend when I was eighteen. I still liked him, of course, from earlier Venture Scout events, but I had never expected him to notice me. I went caving with the Venture Scouts one weekend in the Forest of Dean. The cave was called Great Ham Mine and included some tight squeezes, low ceilings, and a chimney climb. Nigel came along as a leader, as he was home from sea at the time and we needed more adults. I was one of the older Venture Scouts, so I took it very seriously and was enjoying helping the younger ones even though it was very claustrophobic! When we came to the chimney climb, Bob, our leader, decided that he had better not go up first, as he wanted to help the younger ones up, and Nigel was too afraid to go first. I wasn't very impressed with his leadership skills at that moment, so I volunteered to go first. I climbed up and sat at the top in the darkness, and Nigel came scraping up second! He sat next to me, called out that he was up so the next person could start, and then placed his hand over mine in the dark, as if by accident. I didn't pull away but slowly turned my hand over to hold his, and that was it; for the rest of the day, we were inseparable.

After the caving trip, we rearranged people in the available cars so he could take me home, and I was overjoyed. I will never forget the cassette tape he was playing; it was by Genesis, and the track "Follow you, follow me" was playing as our eyes met in the rear-view mirror for a moment, which seemed so appropriate. He dropped everyone else off one by one and then took me to my lodgings with the bassets. We said goodbye rather slowly and reluctantly but arranged to meet very soon. I immediately phoned my mum and excitedly said, "Mum, you'll never guess! I am going out with Nigel!" It was very amusing really, when her reply was, "Oh yes, dear, where are you going?" She then warned me that he was the sort of young man who was charming to everyone and made anyone he spoke to feel special, but I wasn't warned off.

It was the start of a wonderful time for both of us, and we quickly realised how serious we were about each other, and when Nigel proposed the next January, in 1985, my happiness was made complete. We married when I was just nineteen, and he twenty-five, in October 1985.

Jeremy also married his girlfriend, Pamela, in the same year. She was a divorcee who was older than him, and they lived locally to Mum, like we did. They went on to have two children, both girls. He later divorced and remarried, adding another two children to his family: a longed-for boy and another girl. He desperately wanted another son, but his second wife, Edith, had said that she couldn't guarantee him another son and that she didn't really want to have another child, and then maybe another, just to provide Jeremy with another boy. She told him he should be satisfied with his lot! I liked Edith immediately when I met her; she was so down to earth. She was not exactly pretty, although when Jeremy described her to me one day as being built "like a brick shithouse", I thought his choice of words were extremely odd for a man who obviously thought his new wife was a goddess on earth! Edith was an amazing sister-in-law. She had two horses and was the UK rep for Equine America. She loved animals as much as I do, and they had dogs, cats, and rabbits too. I didn't see much of them, and so I was shocked and saddened when I invited them to a 'winter sunshine' party at our house in January of 2016 and she said that she thought I knew that Jeremy had walked out in April of 2015 and she didn't know where he was.

Jeremy's eldest daughter, Amelia, at the tender age of eighteen, made him a granddad at the young age of forty-five, which we teased him about, but he now has two lovely grandsons, Robbie and Larry, and Amelia has now got married—although not to Robbie's father, who was a rather immature boyfriend who had asked her to marry him and whose "ring" she had worn—a red plastic ring out of a cracker. They lived in a little flat, but when they realised that Amelia was pregnant, they bought a small house. Robbie was a lovely baby, but Amelia was a very young mother, and her boyfriend went out to work at all hours, as he was a computer expert who was often on call and out all night. Amelia had no idea how to keep her house clean; it was a pigsty, and she lived on biscuits and cans of soup during the day when her boyfriend was at work, and he cooked dinner every evening or got a takeaway on his way home from work. Whenever I called round to see her, there would be food everywhere, dirty dishes and empty soup cans all over the side in the kitchen. One day there were four plates of food on the floor in the lounge when I arrived, on which there were the remains of what looked like a roast meal: roast potatoes, carrots, beef slices, and a half-eaten Yorkshire pudding. I'd only popped over to give her a lift to the doctor, as she'd scalded herself the day before and the doctor wanted to change her dressing. I told her she would have done better to put the leftovers in the fridge and make soup for her lunch the next day, and she said that hadn't occurred to her but that she would try it next time.

Jeremy had left Pamela unexpectedly and quickly moved in with a new girlfriend, Edith. Pamela was extremely angry with Jeremy and told me that he had a lot of issues, including being unreasonably angry with the girls; shutting them outside the patio doors at night if they cried and woke him up, and things like that. She also said that Jeremy had told her all about my sexual abuse at his hands and how much she disliked him now. Jeremy then told me that Pamela had done him a favour and that if he had met Edith while still with Pamela, he would have left her anyway—which I didn't really believe, as he had been so happy with Pamela. It was quite a surprise when she kicked him out!

CHAPTER 6

DAD'S HIDDEN SIDE

Having realised that my best friend had been abused by her father, I was cock-a-hoop that my own father, who although very angry and often depressed, had never physically spoiled our relationship, and it was clear he loved me dearly until he died. My mother hadn't fared so well, but I was unaware of this until years later.

After I was married, I went to her one day and asked why she had never told me how good married life was, as I was deliriously happy with my new husband and had found that, although she had told me in detail what to expect and armed me with the basic knowledge I would need when married, she had never spoilt the surprise of how wonderful sex can be with the right person, and I was amazed and grateful that she should have kept it a secret for me to discover for myself.

I was so surprised and shocked when she denied any knowledge of good sex and told me how Dad had literally raped her every single night of their married life together. I just couldn't believe it and asked why on earth she had stayed with him, and she said that she'd desperately wanted children and that this was her only chance.

My mother is the most determined person I have ever met, and it didn't surprise me to learn that after she had Jeremy, she continued to try to conceive until she had me, at the age of forty-one, and beyond, although

I was her last child. She told me she'd had numerous miscarriages before we were born, another one in the two and a half years between my brother and me, and another after I was born as well.

I just can't imagine her misery at suffering the indignity of rape every night throughout her marriage, the agony of so many miscarriages, and a husband who wasn't interested in her as a person in the slightest. Once she had us two children, she stayed with him because that was the thing to do—stay together for the children. It wasn't as if he even supported her financially, and I am so angry with her for just putting up with it all her married life.

She did eventually manage to be free of him when, whilst I was still away at boarding school, he left to live in Hove, Sussex. (I still don't know why he left.) After two years, she was able to file for separation and divorce. He didn't contest it, although he cried whenever I went to see him as he got older; he didn't understand why she'd divorced him. She would never have instigated the divorce herself but was only too happy to finalise it when she got the chance. He remarried later, but his new wife divorced him when she discovered that, although in his seventies, he still expected a wife to give him sex every night. She was in her eighties, and she wasn't prepared to put up with it!

To go back to when I was talking to Mum and all this came out, soon after I was married, I naively said that I was so happy that, although Dad had turned out to be a sexual predator in his marriage, at least he wasn't a child abuser or anything like that. My illusions were shattered when she said, barely able to contain her anger, that he had threatened to rape her own mother, my 85-year-old grandmother, in whose house we were living, if she didn't allow him to do as he liked each night, and that on one occasion he had sneered that the summer holidays were looming and that Jenny would be home soon. I was so shocked at this revelation that I couldn't move.

We were in Mum's bedroom at that point, and she showed me her nightdress that she had worn every night for probably thirty years, which was ripped and mended all up the back from where, she said, he would creep up behind her and rip it off her. We went together and immediately, at my insistence, ceremoniously burnt the horrible thing in her garden. She was still so affected by it that she hadn't been able to relax at night even after he'd died, for fear of his ripping it off her again, but neither had she ever dared to throw it away and replace it.

She isn't one to talk about such things much, as she gets so emotional when it all gets stirred up again, but she did tell me all of that. I felt physically sick to learn of these new flaws in my father's personality—flaws that I had never realised existed. I also felt so grateful that she had protected the two of us, my brother and me, all our lives.

I did speak to my brother about it once afterwards—unbeknown to her, as she'd have been horrified—and he was as bothered as I was. But, of course, I could see then the similarities between him and our father—not to say that he does exactly the same things, but he was very interested in sex at an early age, and I bore the brunt of his curious nature. His own first marriage had broken up, and his ex-wife had hinted at all sorts of things he was doing that made her push him away—not necessarily sexual things, but his naked anger shown towards his children and some unreasonable behaviour. I am not ashamed to say that it made me feel vulnerable. I wondered whether maybe I would be as unpredictable too one day, and I wanted to be a very different person to my father. I do suffer with outbursts of anger, usually as part of my monthly cycle, and I am very aware that I need to be careful at certain times of the month.

Jeremy was able to fill me in on other details about Dad too. I knew that he had had an injury to his right foot; he had only two toes on that foot and so walked with a limp. Jeremy said that Dad had told him how that had come about. He had asked his then girlfriend to marry him, and she had replied that she didn't want to be married to a soldier. Dad told everyone that it was an accident, but Jeremy thought otherwise. Dad had gone into a rifle room above his officers' mess and was cleaning a rifle when it went off. Jeremy was sure he had only meant to injure himself slightly so he could be invalided out of the army, but the rifle room had a metal floor, and the shot ricocheted and took off half of his foot. To add insult to injury, his girlfriend then said that she wasn't about to marry a cripple and walked away.

I remember asking Mum about Dad's other children once. Dad had been married before he met my mum, and he also had Mark, Graeme, and Gail. Graeme, at the age of sixteen, was knocked off his bike by a lorry turning left whilst he was on the inside of it going straight on, and he died as a result of his injuries.

I had quite recently spoken with Mum about Mark and his wife, Ivy, and their children, they had Taryn and Gordon, who were not Mark's sons but Ivy's from previous relationships; their own daughter, Tilly; and, much later on, a boy called Richard. Mum didn't like Ivy. With uncharacteristic venom, she told me that Ivy had had two children by different fathers, and that Mark loved her and wanted to marry her, and that there had been absolutely nothing that she could do about it. I don't remember Dad ever commenting, so perhaps he wasn't there when Mum and I had that chat one day, which was years later after I'd married. Mark wasn't even mum's own son, but she had the protective instinct of any mother contemplating the marriage of a beloved son.

I do remember mum telling me that when I was born, Mark came to see me and was enchanted by me! He'd said something like, "Oh, Dad, how do you make them so beautiful?" I don't remember the rest of what Mum said about that occasion.

When Mum and Dad had married and Mum wanted to discuss having a family, she said that his attitude was one of "been there, done that". He didn't want any more kids and told her, "If you want them, go ahead, but you can look after them." Dad did a lot of fun things with Jeremy as a little boy, but I was always safe on Mum's lap, and she hardly let either of us out of her sight. She said that her sister's husband, Tom, said to her once, when she'd gone upstairs to see why Jeremy was crying, "What's the matter? Did the cotton wool slip?" She was hurt but said that she had been left to cry herself to sleep as a child and that she would not ever do that to either of us.

Dad must have loved me even though he didn't feel the need to have any more children. He always referred to me as his "little love" and said that precious things came in small packages, which I loved to hear him say.

CHAPTER 7

ILLNESS

Nigel had to go back to sea shortly after we had decided to marry, and I was kept busy sorting out our house (which we had found and put an offer on and got; it was very exciting furnishing it with Nigel's furniture from his flat) and also arranging the marriage itself. We'd been to see the minister at our church to discuss having our banns read out at the church where we'd belonged as scout and guide. I'd put a deposit down for the wedding reception and my mum made my wedding dress for me and my bridesmaids' dresses too, after we'd been to choose the material.

I was marrying in white—not strictly appropriate, I suppose, but then Nigel married me wearing his Royal Fleet Auxiliary uniform with a red carnation buttonhole, which he said probably wasn't allowed either! I wanted to marry Nigel in his uniform not only because he looked wonderful in it but also to show the world that I was happy to be marrying a sailor. I went into my marriage with my eyes wide open, so to speak.

My chief bridesmaid, my cousin Nell, wore a deep apricot dress, and the two four-year-olds, Nigel's nieces Lottie and Harriet, wore pale apricot dresses and matching ballet shoes which had been especially dyed by Nigel's sister-in-law, Belle, Harriet's mother, for the occasion.

We'd also decided to have a dog to keep me company when Nigel was away, and so we'd bought a beautiful English springer spaniel puppy whom we'd named Peru. Just before our wedding, Nigel and I were involved in a car accident which wasn't our fault, and neither of us was hurt, but it left us without a car for our honeymoon. We had to hire a car for the honeymoon itself, and Nigel's parents lent us their car for the wedding day itself, which was very brave of them!

With all these stresses to worry us, our wedding day at last dawned, beautifully sunny. Nigel was, to my relief, actually in the country. It was a very close thing, though, since he had been serving on a ship which was stationed down in the Falkland Islands for six months, and he had his leave delayed by a few weeks because the sailor coming to relieve him was ill. Luckily, he did make it in time—just.

We had a lovely day. My dad did manage to give me away, and both he and Mum smiled for the family pictures. We had lots and lots of friends there to wish us well. Our reception passed in a happy blur for me; not surprisingly, I don't remember much about it except for the last song played for us, which was by the Cars and was called "Drive", which was appropriate, as Nigel then whisked me away on our honeymoon. Our first choice for the last song was, of course, "Follow You, Follow Me" by Genesis, but annoyingly our DJ had forgotten that we had asked for it. Our friends, of course, had daubed Nigel's parent's car with all sorts of unmentionables, but as it wasn't ours, we didn't care! We swung around the corner, and the cans rattled behind us until Nigel stopped the car to take them off a few miles down the road.

We stayed in a local hotel for our wedding night, and in the morning we had a rude early awakening because Nigel's dad turned up early to collect his car. It was embarrassing, but I stayed in the room and didn't have to face him myself! Our honeymoon was two weeks spent travelling around the UK in our hired car; we spent a week getting to Hawick, on the borders of England and Scotland, and then we had hired a little self-catering cottage to ourselves for a week, and it was bliss. We had open fires every evening and took long country walks to stoke our appetites for food and each other. Coming home was exciting too, as we collected our now ten-week-old puppy on the way and moved into our new house.

I was keen to start a family straight away, but Nigel wasn't sure, as we were only nineteen and twenty-five, so we decided to wait for a while. We still had to get used to being apart a lot, it was true, and Nigel had to go back to sea quite soon after we got home from our honeymoon. He went straight back to the Falkland Islands, so there was absolutely no chance of any stolen weekends together.

I decided to keep myself busy by going back to college and learning to type and to write in shorthand. I did very well and passed lots of exams in secretarial skills during that year and the next, and then I started temping so I could work full-time while Nigel was away and decline when he was at home. I did all sorts of different jobs; some were secretarial, but my favourite was working in the hospital laundry section, folding clean laundry and listening to the radio all day. It paid really well too! It was a master plan and worked beautifully, keeping me busy all the time Nigel was away but leaving us both free to enjoy his leaves.

When we were about twenty-three and twenty-eight, we did decide to start our family, and I arranged to stop taking the contraceptive pill as soon as Nigel next went back to sea for the next six months so that I would have had that period being free from the chemicals and would be ready to conceive (I hoped) straight away on his return. It was an exciting time for us both, and he went off to sea leaving me a little excited and not so upset as I usually was to see him go.

He had been gone only a week or two, and I knew that the ship was just about to sail from the South of England on its way to the Falkland Islands, so I was very surprised one Sunday afternoon to get a phone call from Nigel. He said he had taken unwell on the ship. He had done a week's course as a medic, and so, amusingly, was the ship's doctor, and he said he'd read up about his symptoms and had self-diagnosed either appendicitis or a kidney infection. He said that he had been taken by helicopter off the ship to hospital but that I didn't need to worry, as he would probably just have his appendix taken out and go back to the ship a week later.

The next morning, I was about to go to work, as I had accepted a secretarial temping job locally, when I felt I should phone the hospital to check he was OK, though I was sure he was. I spoke to a nurse who said, "Oh, I am glad you've phoned; I was just about to call you. Could you pop down to the hospital today do you think?" Well, to "pop" down to Weymouth, which was at least an hour and a half away, was quite an achievement in the time I did it and the state of mind I was in, and I don't even remember driving the distance; I just remember phoning my job to say I wasn't coming in, phoning Nigel's parents to tell them I was going down to Weymouth, and then arriving at the hospital. Nigel was sitting up in bed with a huge sticking plaster on his chest. He calmly said he'd just had a bone marrow sample taken but I wasn't to worry. My immediate thought was "A bone marrow sample? That sounds like leukaemia" …, which I just as immediately dismissed as fanciful and impossible—*Not my Nigel.*

He was thinking the same, of course, but didn't voice his fears to me, so we spent a worried couple of days in unhappy ignorance, me going out and finding things to do and then going in to be with him during visiting hours. On the Tuesday, Nigel had telephoned the ship to explain that he was likely to be in hospital longer than he'd thought, and the captain immediately offered me a bed on the ship so as to be amongst friends instead of in an impersonal boarding house, which was what I'd found quickly when I realised I wasn't staying for a very short time. Later that day, I gratefully went to the ship and was met by the guard on the gate who called out, "Cheer up, love; it might never happen …!" He was then so embarrassed to realise that I was the person he had been told to expect to arrive in floods of tears. I held it together, even managing to go to dinner on board with the other officers as usual and to go and see the captain afterwards, because he said he had invited a friend of Nigel's over from another ship, whom he thought I'd know. I didn't even recognise him at first in my shocked state, and I later realised that he had actually been at our wedding with his wife; but of course, he completely understood.

On the Thursday, we were seen by a consultant at the hospital, and he told us that, as we'd both secretly feared, Nigel had leukaemia. In fact, to give it its full name, he had chronic myeloid leukaemia (CML). The doctor explained that, from his experience, it would seem that Nigel had probably had CML for about a year and that he had only about two years left to live without a bone marrow transplant. Without a successful transplant, the disease would progress to acute myeloid leukaemia (AML), for which there was no cure. Even if Nigel survived, he said, it was very unlikely that he would work at sea again. We both sat in stunned silence, clinging to each other. Neither of us could speak, and after a short while we were offered a cup of tea and told to go and talk about it and come back when we felt able to ask questions.

We later found that to have a successful bone marrow transplant, Nigel needed a perfect match, ideally a brother, who was, again ideally, younger than himself. The consultant didn't hold out much hope of finding a donor quickly enough, but Nigel has two brothers—Danny, who is older, and Samuel, who is younger. All those we knew quickly got themselves tested, my own brother being first in line to volunteer, but he wasn't a match— and neither was I, of course. Nobody unrelated was able to help, and in his turn, Danny wasn't either, but then we heard that, amazingly, Samuel was an absolutely perfect match and very happy to donate. We had a long way to go, but now there was hope. We clung to that as we cried ourselves to sleep each night, and it was a dreadful time.

After a while, Nigel had stabilised enough for me to be able to take him home from the hospital in Weymouth, and he was transferred to the care of a more local hospital—Queen Elizabeth's in Birmingham. On the journey home though, after we'd made a detour off the motorway to visit some shops, Nigel got increasingly unwell, and I ended up diverting to his parents' house for help. We phoned the doctor from there and were told to just let him rest, and we went on home later that day to our house when Nigel was feeling stronger.

Nigel and Samuel undertook a battery of tests to see just how compatible they were, and Nigel was fitted with a Hickman line to enable the doctors to take blood and give medication easily with a lower risk of infection. We were told that the treatment for leukaemia was very aggressive and must be started immediately, and that it would render Nigel sterile. This was another huge blow, as we had momentarily forgotten all about wanting to have children, but we were advised to store some sperm now to use later if possible, and to have IVF treatment when we were ready. This we did, and Nigel stored two or three samples, which would have been ample except that it was already damaged by the treatment he'd started, and we were warned that it was probably of no use.

During all this time, we'd decided that it would be best if I looked for full-time employment, as Nigel was going to be in and out of hospital and was probably going to have to retire from his job. We both felt that to get through the times ahead I needed a life of my own, besides caring for Nigel. I quickly got a job as an assistant in the office of a furnishings store in the town where we lived. At the interview for the position, I had realised that I knew one of the people interviewing me; she was a lady I'd known for years, as it turned out! She recognised me too; she knew of my troubles and helped me through the interview. She knew my mum well too, because she was a Guide commissioner whom I had met before at lots of camps and trainings as a patrol leader with my Guide company. Once I was safely employed by her company, she was then very supportive, giving me time off as necessary to be with Nigel in hospital whenever he needed me to be there, and I was also very well trained in the art of bookkeeping and really enjoyed my work, which kept my mind from dwelling on Nigel and our uncertain future.

I loved my new job, and I visited Nigel almost every day after work, sharing the visits with his mum. When I arrived for my times with him, he was often too tired to want to do anything much, as his mum would have played Scrabble or cards with him all afternoon, so I would just sit on his lap instead. All his hair fell out—gradually at first, and then very quickly. He was covered with dry red skin and was very swollen; his poor face was blown up like that of a hamster with full cheek pouches. Every time I went in, I was warned that he looked a bit worse, but I really didn't notice; we were always cuddling and canoodling like any other young couple. The nurses used to laugh and tell us to draw the curtains, as they said it was embarrassing for them to always see us hugging and kissing, but then they always said, as I left after each visit, that I always made his day and it helped him so much just for us to be normal together. Nigel was in splendid isolation in a small room sealed off from the world, but he was fine about that. He really didn't mind a bit, as he was so used to being in small spaces on ships for weeks on end!

We were ever cheerful; Nigel laughed at me because I had to wear a really silly blue netting hat, slippers, and gown whenever I went into his room, and everything had to be sterilised before he touched it, but it soon got to be routine. The day of the transplant arrived and was amazingly uninteresting. Nigel told me he had spent a few hours crammed into a tiny plastic tank, covered with sandbags over his main organs and genitals, being zapped by radiation aimed at his spleen to kill off all his own blood marrow cells. He was soon back in his isolation room, being given what looked like a normal blood transfusion by drip. I had arrived just in time to see Samuel being wheeled back to his ward and Nigel being hooked up to the drip machine. He pointed to it and grinned and said, "That's it—my new bone marrow!" It was astounding that the contents of that little bag of dark red goo were going to make their way into Nigel's sternum and calves (where bone marrow is normally made), having gone through his Hickman line in his chest, and were going to make him well.

Nigel's mum was also at the hospital that day, and she was torn between her two sons going in opposite directions to their wards! There were two other isolation rooms just like Nigel's, and we knew the other inmates; I soon got to know all the other partners quite well too, but they were all understandably very frightened. They all seemed to be alone in their distress and unsupported, while we were surrounded by the well wishes of so many friends and even the people at our church, where we had been so recently married and where Nigel's parents worshipped regularly. We received cards, letters, gifts and flowers from people we'd sometimes never even heard of, telling us that they were praying for us, and we felt brilliantly supported.

Nigel broke all the records for speed of escape from his "prison" and was on a normal ward just six weeks later. He was able to come home amazingly quickly, and I shipped the dog out to kennels and cleaned the house from top to bottom. I even got the car valeted. I have photos of Nigel over the next few months; one is of him doing the cooking in the kitchen, with next to no hair—just a few wisps. To see the photos now is so surprising, because he looked just dreadful, but I can't remember noticing at the time. Gradually, and with a few scares along the way when he occasionally got infections and had to go into our local hospital to see Dr Radley, the blood doctor, he recovered and began to look more normal.

Eventually he recovered completely and even went back to work—not back to sea at first but in London in the Royal Fleet Auxiliary's office, staying in lodgings there each week and having a great time being back to relative normality. Gradually, I got used to him deserting me again, even resenting it if I'm honest, and he worked in the office for two years.

Then he dropped the bombshell that he intended to go back to work at sea. I couldn't believe it. Everyone else was rejoicing that he was well enough and had confounded all his doctors, and I just felt that he was leaving me after all we'd been through; I was devastated.

CHAPTER 8

IN VITRO FERTILISATION (IVF)

In 1992, once Nigel was quite well again and had settled back at work going to sea as before, we decided to go ahead and try to have a baby. We knew he was probably sterile by now, so we contacted a hospital in Birmingham, and we tried IVF, using Nigel's frozen sperm. I had to have all sorts of chemicals so I would ovulate at the right time, which was a nightmare. I hate injections, and I had to have lots. I started with a tablet of hormones each evening which were supposed to make me produce lots of extra eggs that month, and then Nigel had to give me a series of injections each evening, into my thighs, which were of hormones to ripen the eggs. He had to chase me around the bedroom for all the wrong reasons!

On one particular day, I had to go into hospital for a further ripening injection and for the harvesting of the eggs. This was very uncomfortable; I was given drugs to calm me, but I had to lie with my legs in stirrups and a lamp shining into my vagina whilst the long tube was inserted inside me and each egg was collected. I was supposed to have made just a few more eggs than usual, but the doctor stopped harvesting when he got to thirty; I had massively overproduced. No wonder I was so uncomfortable. The eggs were washed and placed equally into two containers, one containing Nigel's thawed sperm and the other containing some sperm from a sperm donor just in case Nigel's sperm had perished. He was chosen for his likeness to Nigel, although of course we had no idea who he was.

I reacted badly to all the drugs I was given and was far too unwell to have any fertilised eggs introduced that day, but we later learned with joy that thirteen of the donor's sperm had successfully fertilised my eggs; this was tempered with sadness because not one of Nigel's sperm had worked. The thirteen donor embryos were frozen until I was feeling better. We had such high hopes for those embryos, and I went back later in the month for some of them to be inserted into my womb. Maddeningly, we found that most of the embryos had not survived being frozen, which was a huge blow, but three precious ones had. The doctor decided I was too small to risk having a triple pregnancy, so he inserted just the two best embryos.

We hardly dared to hope, but I spent a month feeling as though I was pregnant. My mind was concentrating on my tiny twins with delight, but I was trying to keep calm and not worry. When my period started heavily a week late, I knew that we had just lost our only chance of a child. I was inconsolable. Nigel, however, wasn't really surprised, and he didn't react (at least not to me) at all.

CHAPTER 9

DAD

In 1993, my father died. He was seventy-six and ill, not so much physically by this time, but very much so mentally. He had been living on his own ever since he left mum when I was about sixteen to live, at first, in Hove, Sussex. I've no idea what he was doing there, and he seemed to move around quite a lot. For a while he was in Rochdale, but he wasn't at home with me, so I wasn't particularly worried about him.

I saw him occasionally; he eventually moved back to Leamington and had a small flat with a warden keeping an eye on him, and I visited him sometimes. I would have liked to spend more time with him, but he was totally self-centred and only wanted to talk about himself and how hard his life was. I would get graphic descriptions of how constipated he was and what he did about it; he thought it was funny to say he was a constipated accountant these days and was "working it out with a pencil", which was enough to turn my stomach. He didn't eat properly, usually just opening a tin, heating it direct on the hob, and eating it from the tin, thereby saving himself having to do any "women's work", such as washing up.

When he first moved into his little flat, Jeremy and his wife Pamela were doing his laundry for him, but Jeremy soon sorted out a washing machine for him to use himself. No one was surprised, however—least of all Mum—when we discovered (by the smell in the flat) he had left his first load in the machine wet for weeks until it stank, and he seemed genuinely surprised that it hadn't magically gone from the machine to his drawer all by itself.

When Nigel and I became engaged to be married in January 1985, Nigel wanted to be traditional and ask my dad's permission to marry me, so we went to see him specifically one day. However, Nigel was so obviously squirming with embarrassment because of how Dad was living that it wasn't even mentioned, and we left quite quickly. I knew that Dad did want to come to our wedding, though, and he was delighted when I later asked him to give me away in the proper way. Nigel's parents are both quite elderly but are still together and both very healthy and happy, and I think Nigel was quite appalled at how my family behaved.

While Dad was living away on his own, he had struck up an odd relationship with a young lad who was also lost and didn't know what he was doing either. Dad had begun to give this lad, Steven, anything he thought he needed that he had, and Jeremy and I were amazed at how much stuff he had seemingly already given away to him. It wasn't as if Steven needed any of it, and as far as we could see he was just selling everything. Mum had always complained that Dad would sell anything for a quick buck, which he then spent on alcohol, and now we found he was giving it all away too. Steven had even asked for Dad's accordion, which had been his pride and joy when he was younger and which he could play well, and Dad said he was going to give it to him. Jeremy found out, stepped in, and said, "No way." If Dad was going to give his accordion to anyone, it was to be to Jeremy! Jeremy then began to take anything of value home for himself so Steven wouldn't get it. Steven eventually lost interest once the free stuff had dried up and he cleared off, leaving Dad alone again.

I continued to visit Dad occasionally, and then he moved to a block of flats with support for the residents, where he didn't have to do anything for himself. I thought he would be OK there and that they would telephone me if they needed me or Jeremy, but I very quickly learned that he had tried to kill himself a few times there, and he was soon asked to leave, as they said he was too high maintenance. He had been found behind a door with slashed wrists once too often.

On one of my visits, I spoke to Dad about Nigel's illness and then about our attempts at IVF to conceive, hoping for him to be interested and supportive, but to my dismay he was angry with me. He said he had had enough illness of his own and enough baby talk from Mum over the years and that he didn't want to know.

He then moved to a British Legion home, as he was ex-army *and* ex-RAF, so he was entitled to stay there, and it should have been perfect for him. They very soon said that he didn't fit in with them, and they chucked him out again, which I was livid about. He couldn't help being mentally ill, and I didn't think they should have had a choice about helping him. Jeremy told me later that Dad had been trying to have sex with all the female residents and that he was considered by them to be a sexual abuser.

He then moved to live in another small town nearby, in a lovely house with lots of rooms for residents and a warden keeping an eye on everyone. I didn't see him much after that. I did go a couple of times; I loved to see him, and he seemed clean and warm and happy, and he was always delighted to see me, but he never had anything he wanted to talk about or do, though, and was just as happy to see me leave each time so he could go back to watching the television. He seemed to be prepared to live forever like that, and I was quite content with his situation.

I got a call from Jeremy on February 10, 1993, to say that Dad had died in the night. He said that he had been right there with him, and that he thought it was heart failure which had killed him. I wasn't all that surprised, but I was so annoyed with Jeremy that he hadn't bothered to call me sooner. He had obviously received a timely phone call, but I hadn't, so I didn't get the chance to go over in time to say goodbye too.

Nigel was away at sea and couldn't come home. Dad's funeral was held at the crematorium, and although I went along and even sat on the front row with Jeremy and his family, the vicar taking the service didn't even acknowledge me when he came along the row after the curtains had closed, commiserating with Jeremy and Pamela and their daughters; I was totally ignored, and nobody even noticed, which hurt a lot.

The service started late. Our half-brother, Mark, had said he was coming to the funeral service, but he didn't arrive in time in the end, and so we went ahead without him. Mark eventually arrived at Jeremy's house afterwards, apologising for the traffic and so forth, and the wreath he had brought was displayed in their house instead, so as not to waste the flowers.

I don't remember very much about anything after that; I was quite numb with the shock of Dad's sudden death, and then his funeral. Years later, when I mentioned it to Jeremy, he said he *had* realised I was being cut out of the proceedings of the funeral and was ashamed that he hadn't done anything about it at the time. At least recently, when I asked him about Dad's death again, as Nigel needed some information for a security clearance form that he was filling in, he was able to tell me the date of Dad's death straight away—a fact I had completely forgotten.

CHAPTER 10

PARENTHOOD

Nigel and I, resigning ourselves to not becoming parents, moved into our present house at the end of February 1993. Our new house, on the other side of the same town to our tiny cottage, which was by the racecourse, was much bigger, with four bedrooms and a large, airy lounge and main bedroom. The hall had huge windows, and we had two lovely gardens, one at the front and another at the back.

Amazingly, and totally unexpectedly, I discovered in October 1993 that I was pregnant!

Nigel had recently come home from sea, and we had been out celebrating his homecoming and our eighth wedding anniversary, which was coming up at the end of the month, and the next morning I awoke with such painful breasts; I was immediately and irrationally certain that I had conceived the night before. Nigel, of course, ever sensible and not about to get carried away, said that it just wasn't possible and we had probably just overdone it a little. I waited a week or so, until I was late for my period and still had very sore breasts, before I asked my doctor for a test.

He was sceptical too but arranged for the test to be done. I took a urine sample into the hospital and waited. I hadn't done my own test, as the kits are so expensive; Nigel had forbidden me to waste any money on one, because he was so sure I wasn't pregnant, and I suppose he didn't want me to have my hopes raised unnecessarily. I waited for the phone call, which didn't come quickly enough, so I phoned the hospital myself and was met with an airy, "Oh, yes, you are pregnant!" Nigel was away on a residential course that week, so I went out and bought a tiny pair of corduroy blue booties and put them in a little white paper bag to present him with as I met him from the train. He looked into the bag and saw the booties and looked at me in shock and said, "You *are?*"

I wanted to tell everyone, as I was so excited that I had conceived completely naturally. Nigel, although delighted of course, was less overexcited and wanted me to wait at least until the twelve-week scan which had been booked. However, I wanted my friends and family to know straight away in case I lost my precious baby; I needed to know that they were all aware of the situation and therefore would be there to catch me if it all went wrong. Everyone asked the same sort of question: "Was it a natural conception or another attempt at IVF which worked?" They were all astounded that it was a completely natural conception—no one more so than I was though!

We told my mum and Nigel's parents first; Nigel was so embarrassed (and so was I!) when we told his mum, as she immediately asked if it was an "accident" and then was embarrassed at her insensitivity. But we knew what she meant; it was all very sudden for them after Nigel's illness and recovery. They were in shock too, I think, as it was so unexpected.

My pregnancy progressed without incident; my consultant at the hospital allowed me to have as many scans as I wanted to, as he said this was a "miracle" baby. The nurses doing the scans were less impressed, and at the third scan they exasperatedly wanted to know what exactly they were supposed to be looking for, as I had more scans than most mums do. They were very confused when I said that it was just so I could see my precious baby!

Nigel came home from sea just before Charles was born and came with me to my last few scans and check-ups. It was a hot summer, so we were both wearing bright-coloured shorts and T-shirts, and the nurses always laughed at the sight as we walked in, me with my huge multicoloured bump!

I had met a new friend, Carly, during my pregnancy because we went to the same prenatal classes and she lived nearby. We were both due to give birth on the same day, so we had lots in common and spent lots of time together. She had her daughter two weeks early, and Charles went ten days overdue, so in fact the babies were born three weeks apart. We had originally (and unknowingly) chosen the same name as they had in case we had a girl so when their Charlotte was born, we had changed our girl's name to "Emma Louise". We had chosen "Charles Alexander" for our boy's name.

Our son was born in the summer of 1994. It wasn't a pleasant labour; although Nigel was there with me, he just read his paper and didn't talk to me much at all, so I felt as if I was struggling on my own. I had been induced twice with gel to get the baby on his way, and I was nearly ready to give birth, but I was still on the main ward in a lot of pain with each contraction. The contractions had got so close together that I couldn't even speak, and the tears were silently running down my cheeks. I was lucky that a passing midwife noticed, because Nigel didn't! She asked him how long I had been like that and he admitted he didn't know. She deftly checked with her hand to see how dilated I was, and I was rushed through to the labour ward. Things went quite quickly then, which resulted in my having to have an emergency episiotomy (having my vagina cut to get the baby out quickly) without any anaesthetic because there wasn't time; the midwife said that the baby had begun to show some distress and then had passed a bowel movement (meconium) in the womb. He was born straight onto my stomach, which I hadn't expected, and it was horrible! He was grey and wet and hot and slimy, and I wanted him off quick! Once the umbilical cord had been cut and the placenta had been passed, he was rushed over to a paediatrician, who used a tube to suck out the fluid in his airways and stimulated him for what seemed like hours before we heard him cry for the first time.

I then had to be sewn up again. I found myself back in those horrible straps, like when I'd had my eggs harvested during the IVF. The young doctor who was sewing me up airily gave me a painkilling injection before he started, which hurt a lot itself, never mind the needle he then used to sew me up. He told me that I wouldn't feel a thing, but it was agonising. I was still high on the gas I had been breathing for the birth, and he gave me a bit more, so although it hurt an awful lot, somehow I found I didn't mind too much. I kept telling him that I could feel every stitch and it hurt, but he didn't even believe me. He was very arrogant and kept telling Nigel that it was the gas making me talk, but if I could have reached, I would have slapped him. It was horrible. I had a bath after that, with Nigel's help, and when I washed myself underneath, I thought I had a sanitary pad stuck and tried to wash it off before realising it was my very swollen self.

The midwife who had delivered me was very impressed by my huge and healthy placenta, which weighed exactly the same as Charles himself did—a whopping 3.5 kg (7.5lb). She asked if she could take it to show some trainee midwives.

We then spent the usual (in those days) four days in hospital for me to recover from the birth and for Charles to settle, although actually he was placid and calm straight away. We thought maybe it was the effect of the painkilling pethidine injection I had had, which was probably still in his system, but he remained that way until we were discharged and carried on afterwards too. The nurses on duty thought he was marvellous; he hardly ever cried and was often awake, curious and alert all the time. He breastfed naturally and easily, and I recovered quickly.

We were able to walk home on the day we were discharged from hospital, although we had to get special permission to do so, as the nurses all had instructions to not let a baby leave the ward without seeing it safely strapped into a car seat. We had been lent a beautiful Silver Cross pram by a neighbour to use, and we wanted to walk home with Charles settled in that instead. That afternoon we went to a special do with our Scout and Guide group; we were celebrating fifty years of the group. Nigel had been to the anniversary ball the night before, and so everyone knew that Charles had arrived. They were all excited to meet our baby son, and we had a lovely afternoon.

I was rather overwhelmed once we actually got home again though; everything was daunting, and I didn't have any energy to do anything except feed Charles and sleep. Nigel, of course, was busy and doing everything else, but I knew he wasn't going to be home for very long before he would have to go back to sea, so I tried to get up to speed, but nothing worked. I got more and more tearful and worried, which everyone said was quite normal, and Nigel fielded visitors to keep the house quiet.

My mum came to stay to help out a bit, but instead of helping, I just wanted her to go away. I found her quite a threat; she often held Charles close, and one afternoon whilst holding him, he nuzzled her, looking for milk, and she held him closer and announced delightedly that she would get milk herself at this rate and feed him for me. She was remembering the dogs and their sharing of the puppies, and I couldn't get him off her fast enough and was so angry.

I was trying desperately to do everything myself, and one afternoon Nigel suddenly burst into tears after saying he would change Charles's nappy and I said that it was OK; I would do it. He said he felt I didn't trust him, and he was so upset. I was confused at my anger towards him and everyone else, because I had thought I was managing well and doing all that I needed to and more; I was feeding Charles in the night and then, not being particularly sleepy, getting on with hanging out washing in the dark (because Nigel always did it first thing in the morning and I wanted to do it myself), ironing till all hours, cleaning the bathroom at 1.00 a.m., watching Jobcentre Plus television at midnight to see if there was a job Nigel could get locally so he could stay at home.

I asked him once if £19,000 was enough to manage on, as there was a local job he could go for, but he was angry and said of course he was going back to sea and of course that wasn't enough. I had no idea how much he earned, but it seemed a fortune to me. I knew I wasn't well, but I also felt I had no right to be unhappy. I had a lovely, easy baby; a loving husband with a good job; and everything to look forward to.

However, worryingly, I soon began to feel that everything was *too* perfect and that I didn't want it to ever change. I remember feeling strongly one night, when everyone else was asleep, that if the world just stopped now, no one would ever be unhappy again and we would all die happy. I even thought about how I could make the world end, at least for our family. I thought seriously about smothering everyone in their sleep and then killing myself somehow, since then everyone would then die happy and never have to worry about anything again.

Over the following few days, I began to imagine what it would be like if, when out walking with Nigel and Peru, we dropped Charles into the canal. What would he look like under the water? I was very afraid to be on my own with Charles, because whenever I was, these feelings came back, and I thought about harming him and myself. Nigel promised not to leave me alone or, when he did, to make sure someone else would come if I needed someone. He even asked his mum to be on standby, although I felt, perhaps irrationally, that he had asked her only to shut me up.

My doctor was worried about me and wanted me to go into hospital for a short while, but I knew (in my head) that if I did, I would lose both Charles and Nigel forever, and so I wouldn't do it. One day when Nigel wasn't there, I began to feel afraid, so I phoned his mum as arranged to ask her to come over, but she said, "Oh, what is it *now?*" in a cross voice. She said that I was fine, that I should pull myself together, and that she had a life too, and then she hung up on me. So I took Charles for a walk to clear my head, and when we got home, I went to get him a drink, but I suddenly realised that if I went into the kitchen, I would have to pass the knife block, and I could hear it calling to me...

Charles, naturally, began to cry and I went to go to him, but I found that I couldn't enter to the lounge, as I was so terrified of what I would do. My breasts were in agony because I wanted to feed him so badly, but I was stuck in the hall. I was petrified, but I suddenly remembered my lovely doctor, so I phoned the practice (heaven only knows how I knew the number; I just dialled without thinking) and tearfully explained who I was and that I thought I was suffering from postnatal depression and I needed help not to hurt my baby or myself, *now*. The receptionist kept me talking for ages, and suddenly there was a squeal of brakes outside, and there was the doctor on the doorstep! I was so relieved, and I felt better immediately. I was able to let him in, make us both a cuppa, and feed the screaming Charles.

I felt such a fool to have panicked, as I now felt much better, but he said he was sure I was suffering from postnatal depression (PND) and needed to be hospitalised. I didn't agree, because I was so afraid that I would lose both my mind and my boys if I was hospitalised. At one stage during the conversation, I had almost convinced myself that Charles would be OK if I left him at home with Nigel, but then the doctor said that of course Charles would have to go with me, so I couldn't do it. I felt that it wouldn't have helped, as in my own mind, he needed to be away from me to be safe.

The doctor did say that he was reassured that I had asked for help at the right time and was now happy to admit to a real problem, so he was reasonably happy for me to stay at home after all, but he prescribed some medication that I could take whilst breastfeeding to help calm my mind. I had to take another medication too, a muscle relaxant, as the first one relaxed my mind but stiffened my body. The doctor said he was a little out of his depth by now and asked if I minded being referred to a specialist consultant psychologist.

I was so relieved and happy to be referred to a specialist; I knew it was a chance for me to talk about all that had happened to me in my life and perhaps break the vicious cycle at last.

CHAPTER 11

MENTAL ILLNESS

I was so exhausted by this time that the doctor decided to give me a sleeping draught by injection so I would sleep for twelve hours and get some rest. I went to the toilet and then had the injection and was, to my utter relief, out cold for most of that day in the spare bedroom. Once I awoke, I was still so dreadfully tired, but now I really wanted to sleep, and I could sleep, which meant that I gradually caught up and at last began to feel more human. I had another of those injections a while later, and this time went to the toilet *after* I'd had it, which was a mistake, as it worked so fast that I collapsed on the bathroom floor, calling for Nigel. He came in from hanging out washing in the garden and helped me to get up. I felt that he was very annoyed with me, and I think that he thought I was putting it all on, but he helped me to bed, and I slept it off. I was so disappointed when I awoke that it hadn't helped as much as the first injection had, and so I didn't have any more.

I was still feeding Charles myself, and apart from feeding him, the next few days passed in a blur for me. Soon I began to take a different medication, prescribed by my new consultant psychologist; this one was an antidepressant, since he too thought I had postnatal depression. They made me feel quite good and more relaxed, but after a while I began to feel too well again—over the top with excitement all the time, doing too much and not sleeping. I felt that I wasn't depressed, so taking antidepressants could only be making me worse! My consultant came to see me often, and one day I told him that I thought I wasn't suffering from PND at all. If I *had* had PND, then I felt that I didn't have it anymore. I tried to articulate what I felt, and I described the way I felt as "post-postnatal depression elation". He took me very seriously and said that, in fact, postnatal elation is very much a recognised illness, not as common as PND and not many people would have heard of it, but he felt I may have hit the nail on the head!

Around this time, I began to tail off with breastfeeding, as Charles was six- months old and beginning to bite me and it was very painful when he did. Charles went onto bottles of formula milk instead, and in between he began to eat other foods, such as rice pudding, baby meals from packets or tins, and mashed-up portions of our own food.

Once I was no longer breastfeeding, my consultant started me on a new drug called lithium, which was supposed to stabilise my moods somewhere in the middle of the two extremes I had been experiencing. It worked well, and I took it for a long time, and we kept adjusting the level until I was stable. I felt quite well, but eventually I lost all extremes of emotion and felt very "flat". I began to feel that there was no point in life if it was as boring as this! I had to have blood tests regularly to ensure that my kidneys and liver were OK. Then my mum told me she'd seen a programme about lithium and how it harms people who take it for too long, so she was very concerned and wanted me to stop taking it. The doctors I spoke to told me that no one really knew about the long-term effects, as it was a relatively new drug, but I was rather put off, and we began a lengthy time of experimentation, finding other drugs that worked as well but had less chance of long-term effects. They all had various side effects, and it was a case of finding which one suited me best. Some made my food taste strange; others made me stiff again, as before; and one took away my libido so dramatically that both Nigel and I complained! We eventually found a new drug called Seroquel, or quetiapine, which was wonderful. Suddenly I felt well, alive and as if I wasn't taking medication at all. The only side effect I didn't like was that it made me very sleepy, which was fine for the night dose, but I had to take another in the morning, and then I was groggy for a couple of hours. In the end, although my consultant said that because I was already on the lowest dose that would work, he couldn't prescribe me any less, he suggested we could try dropping the morning pill and slightly increasing the evening one instead. This worked beautifully, and suddenly I had my life back!

I really began to enjoy life again at last. On Wednesday mornings each week, I arranged to meet my friend Carly at the leisure centre, where we put the children into the crèche and went to the gym. Afterwards we would have lunch at Meeting Point, which is a small cafe owned by the local Baptist church and incidentally run by another friend's husband, so she would meet us for lunch each week too, with her little girl. Charles and I also went to the swimming pool for mother-and-baby swimming lessons each week, and we attended the Jack & Jill playgroup nearby each morning so I could be with my friends there. I made lots of local friends who had babies the same age as Charles, and we all had a great time.

CHAPTER 12

DISAPPOINTMENT

My consultant had by now explained to me that he thought I was suffering with bipolar disorder, which is a brain disorder caused by a lack of certain chemicals in the brain. I had such huge mood swings without the medication. It used to be called manic-depressive disorder, which certainly described how I had felt. It is often triggered by huge life events, such as childbirth, although individuals are born with it and it shows up only after the right sort of trigger. I suppose many people have it, but if they don't give birth or have any other suitable trauma, they don't even know.

I began to feel strongly that I would like another child, and I said so, but Nigel was dubious, as I had been so ill since Charles was born. However, he said that if the doctor agreed, then we could give it a try. I was thrilled and made the appointment. There the doctor said that as he now knew what exactly we were dealing with, he would be able to prescribe appropriate medication throughout my next pregnancy and during subsequent breastfeeding, and he recommended that we just go for it! I was delighted, but to my utter astonishment, on the way home afterwards, Nigel said he really didn't want to try again; he was now quite sure he didn't want any more children, and so he said he would arrange to have a vasectomy. I was completely devastated again, taking it, of course, as a personal rejection; but at the same time, I could see why he was worried. In all my experience of Nigel, he has *always* been right. I reluctantly had to agree that I *did* need to remain well, as we of course had Charles to consider now. The chances of a perfectly normal pregnancy and birth were of course high, but Charles's pregnancy and birth had been fine too, and we hadn't realised the difficulties it would trigger in me, and we were so painfully aware now of what *could* happen. Even with support from my doctor, the chances of losing what we had already got were too high, and so we agreed to quit while we were ahead.

I went with Nigel for his operation and then spent the next few weeks madly trying to conceive before all the sperm still in the tubes died off. Nigel must have thought it was his birthday and Christmas all rolled into one! Unfortunately, though, I didn't manage it, and I sadly had to accept the fact I was to have only one child. I did feel that Nigel had been especially cruel, though. If he had been so sure before we even asked, why did he let me ask the doctor that question? It was lucky that the mood swings I felt then weren't too extreme; amazingly, the medication still kept me stable, even though these were now legitimate mood swings. I was again very angry and disappointed.

CHAPTER 13

CHARLES

Charles was an easy baby; it was just the fact I was feeling very emotional and very up and down that caused most of the problems I had when he was tiny. In the hospital where he was born, he was a very quiet baby. It seemed that everyone else's babies were crying continually, but he was so content. I learned how to breastfeed and had no real problems except that I had so much milk I was afraid of drowning him! I was aware that my nipples might get sore and was worrying about that, and so on the advice of another mum, we got some special cream which was supposed to help prevent that. It smelled nice and was warming to the skin. I put it on and enjoyed the soothing warmness it provided. When I went to feed Charles later on, though, it never occurred to me to wipe it off; Charles took a huge mouthful and immediately spat it out, milk coming from every orifice: his mouth, nose, and probably his ears too! He just screamed and cried, and I was so shocked and felt so awful. I insisted on a doctor coming to check him out, but he was fine, just cross. I worried that I might have put him off breastfeeding. Luckily he was fine about it the next time we tried.

I learned how to change nappies; I had organised a nappy laundering service to supply me with a weekly supply of cloth nappies when we got home but was using the hospital's disposable ones while in there. I found the first few, which were full of very thick, dark green sticky meconium, very hard to manage; it was everywhere and very hard to clean off Charles's bottom. The next few days' offerings, which were of such odd colours, were also rather off-putting. I had to learn to bathe him, with help from a nurse, before we were to be allowed to leave, so we did that, and he loved it. One of the midwives came to me just before we left hospital to go home for the first time, to tell me that he was a special baby, and I said, "Oh, I bet you say that to everyone!" but she said, "No, they are all lovely, of course, but some are just, well, special, and Charles is one of those." I simply glowed; it was so nice of her to say that!

We proudly took Charles home on his fourth day, having borrowed a Silver Cross pram from a neighbour, which was lovely, well sprung, and hugely comfortable—we hoped. To be honest, after a few minutes walking I wished we *had* used the car, even though it was only a short fifteen-minute stroll; I was very tired. We took Charles out that afternoon to a Scout and Guide event; it was the fiftieth anniversary of the group, and all our friends were there—not to mention a doting granny in the form of Nigel's mum. Nigel had been to the celebration ball the night before, and so everyone was waiting to meet Charles. It was a hot afternoon, and as Granny stole him and went off round the field to show everyone her newest grandson, I was worried about the sun, as we hadn't any cream for him, but he was OK.

When we got home again, I took Charles straight upstairs for a nappy change, and on the way down again, Peru, our springer spaniel, suddenly exploded with barking at a cat that was passing outside. I almost dropped Charles in my shock, but to my amazement he didn't react at all. I asked Nigel to come and clap his hands behind us to see if he would startle, but there was absolutely no reaction at all from Charles again. Suddenly we were both worrying, wondering whether he might be deaf. We considered maybe that was why we'd had such a contented baby in the hospital when it was so noisy no one else could sleep. I realised that I'd not seen a startle reflex from him at all, which in hindsight I remembered was partly why everyone in the hospital had kept commenting on how unusually contented he was.

When the midwife next came to visit us, she said I wasn't to worry and that he was fine. She tried to startle him herself, but she got no reaction again. She decided to refer him to the hospital hearing clinic to reassure everyone and to see if he was deaf or, as she suspected, just incredibly contented. Not that we minded which, but we needed to know. I was worried most about Nigel's mum's reaction if her beautiful, perfect grandson might have a problem. Charles's cousin, Juliet, was having problems with her ears too, and it seemed as though she was actually profoundly deaf, so I decided not to tell Nigel's mum until after the tests.

The tests were easy enough; he had electrodes attached to his tiny head, and sounds were played through headphones straight into his ears. His brain reacted perfectly normally, so to relief all round, we found he could hear perfectly after all.

We had another scare when he was a little older, when one Saturday we couldn't wake him from a nap, and when he eventually woke, he just stared into space and we couldn't get any reaction from him. We phoned the doctor and ended up being admitted to hospital for tests. The doctors there were very worried, and they prodded and poked him, but then they told us that he didn't have meningitis, which scared us, because we hadn't even considered that. The doctors decided, after lots of blood tests from a pinprick in his thumb which left him howling, that Charles was probably anaemic, and they prescribed an iron solution to be fed to him via syringe before each feed. This we gave him, along with the Infacol syrup he was also having before each breastfeed, to help stop him regurgitating so much after each feed, which he had also started doing. The iron solution was very messy, and it stained all of his new baby clothes brown before the midwife found out and told us that there was a clear variety for babies that the hospital should have given us. It was too late, though, and all his sweet new baby clothes were ruined by then. I was very cross about that!

We were impatient to get home again as soon as we knew he was OK, as Charles was being christened the next day and we had things to arrange. Charles was christened at our church just before Nigel had to go back to sea, when he was about six weeks old. He was christened in the family christening robe which Nigel had also been christened in. It was a lovely day. We used the top tier from our wedding cake, which was nine years old by then, but it was moistened and fortified with lots of rum and brandy, and decorated by my mum, with the scene from *Winnie the Pooh* of Pooh being stuck in the rabbit hole and all the animals pulling him out iced around the cake. It was lovely.

Nigel came home again when Charles was eight and a half months old, by which time he was sitting up and getting much bigger. We had spent Charles's first Christmas on board Nigel's ship, which had been in port around the UK, with Charles sleeping in the bottom drawer of his chest of drawers.

We began to go regularly to a toddler group when Charles was two, with my friend Carly and her baby Charlotte, who was three weeks older than Charles. Charles immediately began to show odd tendencies; he wouldn't join in with any of the singing games we played like the other children, he was never aggressive if other children got too close to him, as they were if *he* got too close to *them*, and he hated going, but it was wonderful for me and made me many friends locally with babies of a similar age, so we persevered. Nigel was continuing with his cycle of long periods at sea and shorter leaves at home afterwards, and he just fitted in with us mostly.

It wasn't until Charles was just about to leave the playgroup for nursery school at the age of three that he suddenly stood up and sang all the songs right through on his own, just as though he had just been rehearsing in his head and hadn't even tried to sing them aloud until he was certain of the words. He was like that in everything, never seeming to even try at anything until he was sure he wouldn't get it wrong, when my friend's children simply didn't care. He was the same all through his time there, with letters and numbers and games, in which he was totally disinterested until he could do it all by himself. To help him with colour recognition, which he got wrong all the time, Mum and I would take him on colour-coordinated picnics to help with colours and counting and lots of things like that.

The nursery he attended from age three and a half was attached to a little private school and was just ten minutes' walk from our house. Interestingly, all throughout his time in the nursery, as before, he hated to be corrected and never tried anything new by himself. He wouldn't sing the alphabet until he was suddenly word perfect, nor would he count with the others. He never pushed himself forward or complained if anyone else pushed in front of him. He was so placid that people often commented. He had been very late to be out of nappies; I had to force the issue over the holiday before he was about to go to nursery, and we had a couple of weeks of accidents everywhere, but he suddenly got that too, which was a great relief. Once out of nappies, he was reliable, and he never once wet his bed, much to the envy of my friends! Charles contracted chicken pox when he was three, but he soon recovered.

He started full-time school when he was four, in the reception class at the same school as his nursery. The school was a "first" school, taking children until they were eleven, when they had to find another school for their secondary education, but we weren't really thinking that far ahead except to wonder if he would get into the local prestigious public boys' school at age eleven, like Nigel had. At home he was coming along nicely. However, he was very slow to learn writing and counting skills at school, and his teacher often complained that he wouldn't try.

Near the end of the first year he was there, I was summoned by the head, who told me that Charles's table manners were atrocious and that he was spending a large part of each day under his table, and he wanted to know what I was going to do about it. It was a shock to us, as no one else had said anything about either of those problems! Charles loved art, and he won a whole school competition when he was four with a papier-mâché dinosaur he made. He also showed an early interest in animals, insisting on bringing the nursery's guinea pigs home that summer.

The school was shockingly suddenly faced with closure when the head and his brother decided to sell up and buy another school instead, which was in Henley in Arden. The school site where Charles went was in a prime building area and worth an awful lot of money, so they were buying a larger school in another nearby town which would take children from nursery to age eighteen. Most of the children and teachers, we found, were hoping to transfer to the new site, so we went along with it too, although it meant that Charles would have to go by coach every day.

We had taken a while to decide what to do but felt that although he was having some difficulties, he was still very young, the youngest in his class, and we thought he would mature out of it once he was sure of what was expected of him. The idea of his staying at one school for the rest of his education was also very attractive! I walked him to the bus stop each morning, which was further than his reception had been, but he loved to wait each morning, finding miniature worlds in the moss on people's gateposts, and running around racing everyone. Other people would comment on his energy and boundless enthusiasm for everything, and it was a pleasure to wait for the coach each morning. An older girl, also waiting for the bus, began to take Charles under her wing and loved helping him on these journeys.

His new teacher at the new school who had him in year one was very happy with him, saying that said that coming by coach every day was doing him a world of good, improving his ability to be better organised. He was beginning to not leave everything lying around the school, as was his wont, as he now had to collect all his stuff for the bus home each day. She was a wonderful teacher who adored Charles, saying he was her favourite, even though she wasn't strictly allowed to have one! Charles, however, was still having trouble with his letters and numbers, and he was diagnosed as being severely dyslexic and mildly dyspraxic that year, along with being colour blind. His lovely teacher found a college at Oxford University that takes dyslexic people and excitedly told us all about it, as she felt he was bright enough to go there.

He progressed easily into year two with a new teacher who was equally charmed by Charles, and he was doing well, so it was another huge blow to hear that the brothers who owned it had now gone bust and were closing that school too. The teachers and parents formed a group, and we tried to raise enough money to buy the school ourselves, but to no avail; it was closed and sold off.

We decided when we knew for certain that his school was closing that we had to find another private school, since we could afford it and Charles was now doing so well. We had been to look at a school further away and reserved him a place in case the buyout fell through with his current school, which it did, so he started at their infants' site, and he enjoyed a year in their year three class, which consisted of fourteen of the youngest 8-year-old boys.

Charles began to have more problems whilst in this class, one of which was causing him to miss a lot of school. We had been told he would have to have an operation because his foreskin, which had been very tight at birth, was now getting infected underneath, and he had been experiencing lots of nasty, painful bouts and was going to have to be circumcised. He was also bullied and teased, but his teacher said it was his own fault, as he was behaving oddly.

The head, having reassured us that she would provide support for his dyslexia and dyspraxia, turned turtle and now said he was fine and that this was a middle-class excuse for misbehaviour and that he would have to learn to fit in with their "perfect" children. Charles did have a circumcision during the year, which took a long time to heal; and while he was healing, he contracted a second bout of chicken pox, so he was in a sorry state.

The next year for Charles there was to be year four, which wasn't an infant class, of course, but was in the main junior school and required him to board during term time, which they felt would ensure he would learn to behave as they wanted him to. We were alarmed at their attitude and began to have doubts about that school, and when we decided not to let him go up to the boarding school itself, we were reassured when we heard that around thirty other families' children either didn't go up or left year four during the first few weeks of going up. We heard later the head was sacked over her attitude. We had been travelling forty-five minutes each way on our journeys to school that year, and so we looked nearer to home for another school, to give ourselves a break.

We found instead a little Catholic private school, and when we went to have a look around, we were delighted to discover that this was where most of Charles's friends had transferred to on the closure of the other school. The school was only about a ten-minute drive away, and the head there was very sympathetic towards Charles's difficulties; we all felt that he would do well there. He joined their year four class and had yet another teacher. Almost immediately I began to get complaints, as she said that

Charles's behaviour was very odd and sometimes dangerous. For instance, he had made friends with a boy in his class who used a walking frame on wheels and crutches to get around school and had, one playtime, decided to play horses. He had tied the wheeled frame to his waist and careered off down a slope. The alarmed staff, having noticed their antics through their staffroom window, had rushed to the playground in order to save the other boy. They were becoming very concerned about Charles.

Another time I was called in because Charles had managed to break a door off its hinges in the boys' toilets. Charles wasn't where he should have been when I got there, and I eventually found him still in the boys' toilets, cowering where he had been shouted at. He said a boy had attacked him with some drumsticks, but the head had said that *her* children didn't behave like that and disbelieved him. I had had about enough of their accusations, and so we called in an educational psychologist to assess Charles. After a few days of observing him closely, she said that she felt he was displaying autistic tendencies and diagnosed him as having Asperger's syndrome. She actually said, "I hope I'm wrong for your sake, but …"

The head was then very keen to get rid of us, but to her credit, she helped us to find another school for Charles. Her advice was to go to a state school where they couldn't just ask him to leave and would actually help him properly.

We then started Charles at his new primary school just a few weeks into the term. It was just a twenty-minute walk from our house, and from the start he fitted in beautifully. A lot of the children there behaved strangely, and we found he didn't stick out at all. The staff there had all received training to help autistic children, and so he was well supported and, more importantly to us, valued by them, and he blossomed. He progressed throughout his time at this school, firstly in year four with his first male teacher; he then enjoyed year five and he loved being in year six, wherein he did his SATs (Statutory Assessment Tests) exams and he left the school to go to a local comprehensive school, just a twenty-minute-each-way cycle ride for him. Charles left his lovely little primary school and started at this enormous secondary school in September 2005—a big enough leap for anyone. Even so, he was fine and enjoying himself. He was managing to get twelve to fourteen As each week—no mean feat when they are awarded only for exceptionally good behaviour, work, or homework. He got some Xs too, but no more than two in any week, and therefore he had no detentions at all—a record he's very proud of!

His attendance at secondary school was excellent. In the first year it was 100 per cent, and he got a letter congratulating him on that achievement. Big deal, yes, but to have had one that year was great, if only for me! He was very popular with the teachers, as he was almost the only child who wanted to learn, was polite, helped clear up after lessons, and didn't cause trouble.

Sadly, however, Charles was attacked at school during his second term there, between lessons, by a different neighbour's son, Gareth, whom Charles used to be quite friendly with. This boy doesn't like Charles much now, and was horrible to him at school, along with his sidekick, a nasty girl who used to live next door to him in our close. When they were all younger, these two used to attack Charles together. The attack at school was serious enough for Charles to have to go to the head of year to report it to him. He was shown lots of photos of boys called Gareth in the school so he could pick the culprit out so that he could be disciplined. Charles told me about it later on because he was afraid that I would hear that he'd been sent to the head and would be cross with him! He didn't understand that he wasn't the one who'd done wrong.

He was then, alarmingly for me, attacked again, on a different day, on his way home from school; two girls jumped on him from behind and hit his cycle helmet so hard that they broke it. His head was swimming, and he almost fainted. He didn't tell me until the next morning at breakfast, and only then because we were talking about bullies and strangers, and I told him just to kick and shout and make as much fuss as possible so that a passer-by would stop and help, and he said, "Actually, Mum, that doesn't work; I tried it yesterday, and everyone walked by laughing at me."

I phoned the school, absolutely furious, and the head of year, whilst being sympathetic, said that I should have called the police instead, since it was a common assault outside school and that there was nothing much he could do. There wasn't much point in phoning the police, since I had no idea who the attackers were, but Charles was sure they were girls from school, so I asked the head of year for his help, and he said he would get Charles and an older boy to try to find them in school so he could talk to them. Charles never saw them again, and in the end he said that he was only sure they were from his school because "no one else walks through the park at that at time of day, so they *must* be from my school." Charles logic strikes again.

Once Charles had started at secondary school and started going on his bicycle, I had more time at home. I felt elated and happy and started to spiral into a manic-depressive stage, spending all my spare time cleaning. My doctor increased my medication and kept a close eye on me, arranging for a community psychiatric nurse (CPN) to visit me each week. I ended up being signed off work with stress and remained at home for eight weeks. Luckily, I remained well enough to cope at home, and gradually things settled down again.

Charles blossomed at school too, where the special educational needs coordinator (SENCO) was marvellous. He stayed throughout his time there with the same male form tutor and was soon gradually rising up through the sets. Using his SATs results from primary school, they had placed him in set three for every subject, but after the first year, he dropped a set for maths and DT to set four, but he went up to set one for science. The next year he went back up to set three for maths and up to set one in art, music, and drama. Charles finished year seven, enjoyed year eight, and then started in year nine at school, and he still loved it. During the first term of year nine, though, all the teachers had the same complaint—that although his work was excellent orally, no one could read his writing. We went to see the SENCO, and we were delighted when he immediately promised Charles an AlphaSmart (a laptop word processor) the next day, as he had six, four of which were broken but one of which was spare. Charles used this in school until year ten and now had work he could revise from because he could read it. In year ten he progressed to a laptop computer with Internet access, which he was allowed to use for working towards his GCSE exams, and then a school computer for the exams themselves. He had made all of his choices for his GCSEs and got all of the ones he wanted. He studied art, drama, electronics, psychology, and history, along with English literature and language, mathematics, science, religious education, and PE. He absolutely loved being at school there and came out with pretty good GCSE results.

After GCSEs, he went into the sixth form to study physics, use of maths, psychology, and design technology and got reasonably good grades—not as good as we had hoped for, but the results he himself had expected. He didn't take art at the higher level because his teachers had been using reverse psychology and had told him he wasn't trying hard enough, and so he had dropped it as a subject, much to our dismay—and theirs! His art was really brilliant and was what he wanted to make his career in. He decided that he really wanted to go to college next to study for a BTEC national diploma in games development, which he applied for and enrolled in for the next two years.

Charles duly received his end-of-course results, and he waited until the three of us were together before he would tell us he had scored maximum marks for the whole course! He had triple distinction * for his BTEC plus another distinction for his art course. He was officially the top student on his course and was nominated for an award as well; to say we were all thrilled was an understatement!

We went to Charles's end-of-course exhibition, where he showed us the Stalingrad model his group had made. Charles had painted tanks and soldiers at home, so we knew what it was going to be like, but it was really wonderful and attracted a lot of favourable comments from other visitors to the exhibition. He had also decorated their stall for showcasing their game, and that was really smart too.

It was a wonderful end to a busy year; with Nigel's promotion to captain that year too, we were all very, very pleased with how 2013 had panned out. I had suggested that I would like to stop working at the end of the academic year so that I would be free to go to wherever Nigel was in port, but Nigel (right, as usual) said that it wasn't a good idea and that I should continue at least for another year while I got used to being home alone. Once he was settled back at sea, and Charles at university, we would rethink this.

Incidentally, our marriage got better immediately; we had got Charles safely to adulthood, and he had excelled at college, Nigel was near the top of his career tree too, and I was settled on my medication and doing well at work. It was going to be interesting to see how I would manage once both boys had gone, especially at first, but at the same time I was counting my blessings and was not too worried about the future. Nigel and I felt as though we were newly married again and could hardly keep our eyes or hands off each other, which was wonderful.

Charles duly progressed to university, and his friend from college also enrolled on the same course, and his mum was prepared to buy a house for them to share whilst there. Charles graduated with a 2:1 in computer games art, and after nine months of warehousing and temping, he finally landed a great full-time job in the town where we live! He was able to afford to rent a small house on his own, so he moved out, seeing me most weekends for Sunday lunch at our house.

I had had a few hard reminders of how things can suddenly change; a friend on my Christian Moms of Boys Internet group suddenly lost her husband as a result of an epileptic fit one night (at age forty-two), another friend lost her son (at age twenty) when he went missing in Sweden and was found dead the next day, and another friend lost her mum to cancer, all in the same week. It doesn't do to worry about the future; no one knows what it holds, which is just as well, really. Had I known all that was going to happen to me in my life, I'm not sure I would have been able to carry on.

CHAPTER 14

SCOUTING AND GUIDING

I had tried to join Brownies as a little girl, but the pack I started at wasn't very good. We didn't do much, and I was dubbed "Henrietta" as I was so small and had a short name, and they all thought it funny to rename me. I was not impressed! I joined the Guide company at our local church at the age of ten, when we moved there in the summer of 1976. My brother joined the Scout troop, and by the time we had finished, we both ended up patrol leaders. I was patrol leader (PL) for the Blue-Tit Patrol and later the Kingfisher Patrol, and he was PL of the Eagle Patrol. Mum was involved as an assistant Guide Leader too. She had been a member of the Guide Association since joining Brownies herself, and Dad had been a Scout too, so they were keen for Jeremy and me to start as well. Of course, I also met my husband Nigel when he was a Scout, and later when we were both Venture Scouts.

I was a Guide until I joined Venture scouts at age sixteen in 1981. "Ventures" were for all young people aged between sixteen and twenty-one then; these days after Scouts and Guides, you can join Explorer Scouts (for boys and girls aged thirteen and a half to eighteen) or Ranger Guides (which is just for girls and which caters to a similar age range). Jeremy was also a Venture Scout, so we usually went together to meetings. Going to Ventures was great fun, and it was held at our church still, so I could walk up for meetings from home each Friday if Jeremy wasn't there to take me. The leaders were amazing. We did all sorts of things: gardening for other people, tenpin bowling, and playing our guitars together. And each Easter, we went egg-rolling together on local hills. We always spent May Day on top of these hills, watching the sun rise, which was wonderful too. We did a lot of hiking together and camping too.

When I was twenty, in 1985, I was about to have to leave Venture Scouts, but I didn't want to leave the group at our church, so I decided to help with running the Cub Scout section for a while. I worked with the church minister's wife, who was "Akela". I was "Colonel Hathi", and we worked with "Kaa" and "Baloo". I enjoyed my many years working with the Cubs, although I sometimes found it hard, as I was so desperate for a son of my own!

In the late '80s, Nigel was taken ill with leukaemia and I took a break from Scouting, but I was soon called back, this time into the Guiding side of the group at our church, around 1992, where the Guide company needed more leaders. I joined the Guider, who had recently arrived from Australia with her family and was struggling to run Guides on her own. Annoyingly, as soon as I got started alongside her, she decided to leave and left me to it. I managed to quickly recruit a youngster I knew who was wonderful, and we ran the company together for a while. I then discovered, joyously, that I was pregnant in October of 1993, and so I decided to leave the company; another leader had been found, and so I was able to leave when I needed to.

When Charles was very small, just about a year old, a neighbour in our close asked me if I would like to help with running a Brownie pack in Warwick. Of course, I said I couldn't, having such a small baby, but she offered to babysit for him each Monday while I went. Her daughter was a Brownie with the pack, and it was about to close because it hadn't enough leaders, and parents had been asked to either help themselves or to find more leaders as soon as possible! I felt well and able to go, and I thoroughly enjoyed my evenings off once a week. This worked very well for a few years. I enjoyed working with the Brown Owl, and when in due course my neighbour's daughter, Emma, left Brownies, we started a babysitting circle of Brownie parents instead, and as Charles loved going to all the different homes each week, it worked really well.

When Charles was about five, we went to watch the biennial group show, Daley Sketches, at church, as we did each time it was on, and by chance I was told that the Rainbow section would be closing after the show, as they didn't have a leader any more. Of course, I offered to run the Rainbows there and then, rather than see it close, and for a few years I helped to run Brownies in Warwick as assistant Brownie Guide leader (Snowy Owl), and I was Rainbow Guider for the Rainbows at our church in Leamington each week. Rainbows is the youngest group for girls in the movement; girls can join at five and remain until they leave at eight to go to Brownies. I was able to do both because my parents-in-law had offered to have Charles for tea at their house each Tuesday when I went to Rainbows. I recruited another friend to be my assistant Rainbow guider, and at the next Daley Sketches we recruited a parent to come and help, so it went well for a long time. We had a super young leader who came each week, as she had for the previous leader; she was wonderful. I decided to leave the Rainbow unit in 2006 when another friend, who was an assistant Beaver Scout leader with the group at the time, expressed an interest in doing it for girls instead of the boys, as they seemed so much better behaved! I was keen to relinquish the Rainbows and Brownies too, so I stopped them both. By that stage, I had been doing it twice a week for over seven years, and I needed a break.

I was still involved with our group when Charles went through Beavers, Cubs, Scouts, and Explorers. He was patrol leader for the Eagle Patrol in Scouts, as my brother once was too. Nigel is assistant group Scout leader and helps when he's at home, and we help organise special events, and I sometimes used to do the shopping for food for group barbecues and suchlike, as I had a Booker's Card from school.

Nigel and I were also heavily involved with AMSAG, the Association of Methodist Scouters and Guiders. I edited their magazine, *Scattered Leaves*, and Nigel is currently chairman of the group. We joined the association when we went to a conference one year and really liked the people. It was funny, as at our first meeting with them, I felt I had known some of them for years. Indeed, we both felt the same, as they were so friendly. It was only later that I realised with amazement that I *had* met some of them before. I had been at a Guide camp in 1979 with my company, which was run by AMSAG, and two of the older members had been there, and another AMSAG member, the same age as me, turned out to have also been there, as another 14-year-old PL!

CHAPTER 15

STARTING WORK AGAIN

I began looking around for a job as soon as Charles was settled at school and I had time on my hands. Nigel had spotted an advertisement in the local paper for a lunchtime supervisor at a local private school. I applied, went for an interview, and was pleased to be offered the position, although I later realised that no-one else had applied! I started work there and ended up working there for the next seven years with a motley bunch of other ladies, some friendly and others just nosey.

A lady called Jo soon befriended me and showed me the ropes, but the others began to warn me that she was trouble with a capital *T*. She was one of those people who, having not had much experience of certain things—motherhood, for instance—had lots and lots of unwanted advice to give on that subject, and indeed she began to wear me down, always telling me how to deal with Charles's difficulties, so I began to make sure I didn't tell her anything.

The trouble was that another of the ladies, Taylor, had similar problems with her own son, and so we often compared notes. Jo would always eavesdrop and make sure she added her opinions; it drove us both mad. She and I complained to the head about Jo so much that eventually she moved us together, to the other playground, to look after the older girls without Jo there, which was much nicer. Jo began to cover the dining hall after that, so everyone had a break from her (except those unlucky enough to be in the dining hall too!), which was a great relief all round.

I actually quite liked Jo; her heart was in the right place, but she was so overpowering and dominant that she overshadowed every group she tried to join in with until everyone was ignoring her totally. My colleague, Taylor, often still being the recipient of her advice before and after work, finally decided she had had enough and decided to leave the school altogether. She found employment in a nursery and trained as a teaching assistant to work there. The head teacher then offered me the chance to work in the nursery which I jumped at, and it was really nice to be part of a team that actually worked together, and in which everyone was valued.

During my time there, at the head's suggestion, I decided to train for a National Vocation Qualification (NVQ) Level 2 Teaching Assistant Award myself, and I passed with flying colours. There wasn't a position for me there, unfortunately, so instead I applied for, and got, a special educational needs teaching assistant position at another local primary school. I was delighted that it was the very school where Charles had been so happy!

I was still at the private school where I had worked for seven years as a lunchtime supervisor. The previous year, the head of the Pre-Prep Department, had told me she thought that I was "wasted in the playground". She obviously didn't mean that I had been drinking, but she had noticed that I was getting good at spotting children who seemed unusual and who were attracting attention from supervisors and constantly being told off. If ever I went to see her to talk about why she thought Jonny was behaving so strangely, she would smile and say I'd done it again—the child had specific problems. But with the facility being a private school, she was not allowed to share this with staff unless they specifically brought it up. Anyway, she and I would discuss these children, and I helped them in the playground and saved them from the wrath of the unsympathetic supervisors.

I was also still having trouble with adult members of staff in the playground, as we had such different views about how to treat the children in our care. The head arranged for me to work in the nursery as well as on the playground, releasing me from the daily trudge of disagreeing all the time. I worked in the nursery for a year, making myself useful, enjoying the children and staff very much, and discovering how much I liked being in the classroom. I decided that perhaps I would train as a teaching assistant so I could help in the classrooms as the head wanted me to, and I started the National Vocational Qualification (NVQ) course to be a teaching assistant level 2, in January 2006. The course should have cost £670, but under a government scheme called Train to Gain, as I held only four O-levels, I could have the course free. Anyone with five or more had to pay the full cost, but the scheme allowed undereducated people an equal chance to better themselves. Never before had I been so pleased that I had flunked at school!

The course lasted for four terms normally, but under the scheme I had to complete it within three terms, which meant I would finish in June 2006. I felt this was more useful anyway, as it would give me a chance to apply for positions to start in September. At the private school that year, I was given the chance to work with a year one class on Monday afternoons and a year two class on Tuesday mornings so I could gain the experience I needed for the course.

This was a magical year for me; I loved the classroom work, I enjoyed the course, and I wasn't on the playground so much either! I had to take a literacy exam during the course for the college to keep a record of the standard of students doing their course, and I got full marks, which was unheard of! My confidence in myself began to soar. I passed the course with flying colours in June, and then I began to look for a suitable position.

I was pleased to find, on the county council website job page, that Charles's old primary school was advertising for a special educational needs teaching assistant, level 2, to work with a child in year two (so six years old) with a statement and diagnosis of Asperger's syndrome, which is, of course, what Charles has.

I was now on my way to finding the perfect job, Charles was settled at school, and Nigel was happy in his life too. I had discovered what was wrong with me, and I had sorted Charles out too, so now, at last, I felt I could really get on with my life!

I applied for the position, filling in the county council's forms. I ticked the "mental health" box so I could explain about being bipolar. After all, I knew that I would need time off to recover from episodes and that taking a week off at the start might save seven or eight weeks later on in the year. I was called in for an interview with an occupational therapist who said she had never met anyone so clued-up about her own condition, and she passed me as fit to work with children, with no reservations.

CHAPTER 16

ANNIE

I had been a governor at this school while Charles was in years four, five, and six, and I now found that I still knew lots of members of staff. I was called for, and thoroughly enjoyed, the interview at the school, and I was offered the position that afternoon. I was elated. I was to work each afternoon from 1.00 p.m. to 3.15 p.m., mainly supporting the one child but also supporting the rest of the class where I could, with the aim of getting her totally integrated into the class and not needing support by the end of the year. I had a niggling doubt though; if she was to not need me by the end of the year, would I still have a job? The head assured me that there would always be positions for the right person and didn't think it would be a problem. I had to take a leap of faith again and leave a safe job for one I hoped would last me a lifetime! I was also pleased with the hours, as I was so used to working 12.20 p.m. to 2.00 p.m., having to have my lunch at 11.30 a.m. and not being able to eat with Nigel when he was at home, and not having a whole morning or afternoon to myself, ever. Now I could eat at 12.30 p.m. with Nigel if he was home, work all afternoon, and have mornings to myself.

I started my new job full of trepidation. Would the children relate to me? Was I really cut out for this? Would I be able to help them? I needn't have worried. Annie was delightful (most of the time), and I was able to start the process of not allowing her to decide that she didn't want to join in, and I managed fairly quickly to get her sitting still and listening. (It's not that she wasn't listening before, but she was wandering around the classroom fiddling with things, which disturbed the others. I was very aware that she *was* listening but that she was unable to sit still at first.)

Her work was good, she had the nicest handwriting of the class, and her drawings were lovely. She understood the work well and enjoyed doing whatever was set for the class to do. We went through one or two tantrums when I made sure she did as she was told and when I didn't allow her to hurt other children just because they had looked at her in a way she didn't like or had disturbed her games with her friend.

She only really played with one child, a Spanish boy with difficulties of his own, not least that English was a new language for him, and he sometimes didn't understand what was being said to him. Her standard way of coping with a situation she didn't like was to run full tilt away from me. If the door to the playground wasn't properly fastened, she would vanish outside. This was made more dangerous as there were builders in the playground, demolishing a building and building another, so half of the playground was fenced off. Of course, she could slip through the fence while I couldn't, and she would be standing looking into a deep hole when I caught up with her.

The first time she did this, on my very first day, I was so afraid she would hurt herself, and I was acutely aware that the head might be looking and see the situation she was in, so I took a deep breath, lowered my voice and told her to come back to me now. She came back to the fence and slipped back through, whereupon I grabbed her hand and marched her back into school, very relieved.

I talked to the SENCO about these bouts of blind flight, when she could end up anywhere in school. The second time she flew away from me, on only my second day, she went into the bowels of the school, and I was expecting to find her in the assembly hall, as I'd been told she often went there to run around when in meltdown. I found her instead in the kitchens, dancing around the hotplates! I was horrified and sought the SENCO again, urgently needing a way to stop this behaviour. I suggested writing her a "social story", as Charles had had when he was there, for similar reasons, to explain to her why it was important she stop doing this. I wrote the social story and printed it off for the SENCO to see, we adjusted it, and I printed and laminated it that evening.

The next day I showed it to Annie. I read it with her, explaining that I wasn't just being mean and stopping her running away, but that it was dangerous for her to be on her own in kitchens; under the computers in the computer suite, amongst all the cables; in the out-of-bounds section of the playground; or wherever. She took the social story home to look at with her mum. The next day she asked me why the classroom door was so dangerous. She had seen the picture of the classroom door and had been told before that it was dangerous to go through it. She took everything so literally, and I had to explain basic things right from the start.

Gradually I managed to get her to begin to understand; at least the running away began to lessen. She was to be allowed rewards for doing as she was told, but I found these hard to award since she was always doing her own thing. I wasn't sure how much I should physically stop her from leaving the room whenever she liked or being aggressive in the playground. I talked to the SENCO every day she came in, which was only on Tuesdays and Fridays. I must have driven her mad, but she seemed genuinely pleased that I was so on the case and badgering her for approval of how I was dealing with Annie and asking for advice.

I drew up more social stories about Annie listening and doing as she was asked in a lesson, and then she would get a reward, such as the opportunity to play with the play dough, draw, look at a favourite book, or go on the computer for a while. It took weeks before she earned a reward, but once she did, they came thick and fast!

Once Annie was settled, I noticed another little girl who was crying out for attention. Ellie was very quiet and couldn't read or write. I discovered that she had 3 siblings, all younger than herself. She was only seven, and she seemed to be the most mature person in her family; her mother was awful – always coming into school, shouting and screaming about anything she liked. I tried to support her and had some success whenever

Annie was suitably busy and didn't need me for a little while. On one occasion when Ellie had been absent on a Friday, she came to find me in the playground the next Monday for her usual cuddle. I told her I had missed her on the Friday, and she replied that she had had to 'look after the kids' whilst her mother went shopping. I mentioned this to the teacher after break and she told the head. Ellie disappeared after that and I was eventually told that social services had been waiting for such an opening when they could take the children into care. She did return later, clean, well fed and so happy. Now that they were all in care the siblings began to improve in everything – but it was sobering for me to realise that I had been the reason for their going into care.

ANDY

In the second week after I had started at the school in the afternoons with Annie, the head had asked me if I would like to extend my hours to also work with a boy in year three. I was delighted to accept, as it meant going into school only a little earlier, at 12.15 p.m., and helping him over his lunch break for just forty-five minutes each day while his one-to-one helper had her lunch. I went in with Annie as usual at 1.00 p.m. just the same. Of course, that meant a return to an early lunch on my own even when Nigel was at home, but he said he didn't mind.

Andy was seven, and he was described to me as a "found in a cupboard" type child—that is, one who had had no stimulation at all until he was found, at age six, still in nappies, with no language and no comprehension of life other than from watching television and playing Xbox games. He was apparently the youngest of five boys; two of his brothers were aged fourteen and sixteen, and they were at secondary school nearby, and the next older brother, who was about twenty, had already left home. The oldest boy was in the army and rarely at home.

I heard from a child in the playground that there was another even older brother too, but no one else ever mentioned him. Andy's mum was very angry, seemingly at being found out as having Andy at home, but she had no interest at making things easier for him or us, and although she brought Andy to school each day and collected him on time, she never spoke to anyone and was not involved in his care or education at school at all.

The SENCO advised me that Andy was being taught to use Makaton signing to help him communicate, as he didn't talk, and that she felt he was probably on the autistic spectrum somewhere, but no one knew quite where at this point. I was hoping that I would get some training in Makaton signing, since I didn't know how to use it, but this was not forthcoming. The lady who had him all day said she had some sheets on Makaton "somewhere" that she would bring in for me to look at, but this didn't happen for weeks.

Andy was a lovely little boy. He had big brown eyes that were usually twinkling and laughing with him, although they were sometimes very solemn too. Each day at 12.15 p.m., I would find him with his classmates, in the computer suite, completing their maths programmes. Each child had his or her own programme to work through daily, and Andy was racing through his, as his understanding of maths and numbers seemed pretty good. His method of choosing his answer was interesting; instead of choosing the number straight away, he would run his fingers up and down the keys as though he were playing a piano. If the number he needed was a low one, he would start at the high numbers and work down to it, and the opposite if he needed a higher number. He never made any mistakes with addition or subtraction, knowing exactly what he wanted to do, but he always used this odd way of choosing the answer.

As soon as he finished this each day, he would log off his computer and leap off his chair to rush through to get his lunch. It was all I could do to keep up with him at first. He was always so keen to get his tray and cutlery that he would push through the queue and jump to the front, but nobody ever minded, and he would point enthusiastically to his choice of food, smiling at everyone. One of the older boys often saved a place for him in the queue and told me that his own little brother was "like Andy". Andy was very happy for me to cut up his meat if necessary, and he ate very neatly, polishing it all off quickly. He usually started with his pudding, but he ate his main course too, and he was then very happy to take his empty tray and put his beaker and cutlery in the right boxes, thrusting the now empty tray into my hands to put onto the pile of trays while he rushed off to find his favourite friend.

This friend, unfortunately, was a boy who was always in trouble, since he was aggressive and rude to teachers and other staff, and his favourite game was "World-Wide-Wrestling"; he had DVDs of all the big fights, and the games on his PlayStation too. He never tired of grabbing and wrestling younger, weaker boys and hurting them, and then being sent in, to the head's office, and Andy followed him around adoringly.

At first Andy would frantically gesticulate to me while he was eating, signing all the time between bites, and I couldn't understand anything he tried to tell me. I smiled and watched and tried, but it was double Dutch to me! We would rush outside after he'd eaten, and he would follow his friend around, and then, when he was invariably sent in, Andy would go and find some stones and start to throw them across the playground. Obviously this was dangerous, but he was oblivious to anything I said, and it was a difficult thing to stop. We had builders in to repair the school roof and some walls by the playground, so there were lots of stones on the ground.

I had noticed the one thing he *was* always getting wrong on his maths programme was directions, such as "over", "left", "right", and "straight on". In desperation one day, I managed to get him to throw the stones over the fence and onto the grass instead of across the playground, encouraging him to throw over the fence, and then to the left or the right or straight on, reinforcing the terms he was encountering on his maths programme. I knew this still wasn't allowed (the throwing of stones), but I thought this was better than throwing towards the other children. I hoped the caretaker would forgive me when he chipped his mower blades though! I mentioned to the SENCO what I was doing, and she laughed and said she would never have thought of that.

I always had to go in at 1.00 p.m. with Annie and the other infants, meaning that I had to leave Andy to his own devices for fifteen minutes, as the junior section of the school didn't finish their lunch break until 1.15 p.m.. But I handed him over to another supervisor each day and hoped for the best. He was often in trouble and being told off once I had gone in, which he hated because he didn't have anyone to guide him. This was such a shame, as it ruined his afternoon moods.

During lunchtime on my second Monday with him, Andy was signing to me the same thing over and over and looking at me as if I were totally stupid, as usual. He was making an *M* with his index fingers and then an *S* with his little fingers. I eventually shook my head, looked him straight in the eyes, and said, "Andy, I can't understand what you are signing; you are going to have to tell me," whereupon he smiled and said, "It's Monday … I'm going swimming!"

I was so pleased! He *could* talk after all! And he knew enough about English to be able to say what he wanted me to know.

After that, he told me that Monday was swimming day *every* lunchtime, and then he began to say "left", "right", "straight on", and "over" when he was throwing stones in the playground too. I hadn't realised that I was the only person he was talking to until one day when he leapt off his chair in the computer suite to go to lunch as usual and I automatically asked him to say "excuse me" instead of pushing past the children who were lined up at the door as usual, and he did.

The teacher in the room did a double take and said, "He spoke!" I told her what he was saying regularly to me, and after that he began to talk to her too, and his usual afternoon helper as well. Once he started talking to everyone, there was no stopping him. It was lovely how he developed his language skills very quickly. He knew how very pleased everyone was with his progress.

One day he amazed me by saying "classroom", "books", and "toilet" all in one lunchtime. He soon learned the words for his emotions and was able to say "happy", "sad", and sometimes "hurt". He surprised his morning helper one day when she asked him how he felt as he was pulling a strange face, and he said, "Confused!"

Andy had favourite toys in class and began to take them out to play with. He had two hand puppets which were for him to use for role play. He called the boy puppet Jerry (one of his brothers' names) and often told me Jerry was angry, which didn't bode too well for his home life, we felt. Foxy was the puppet he used to throw around; often he ended up on the low roof of the toilet block and had to stay there until the caretaker could get him down again for us. Andy was very rough with him, even pulling his leg off one day. I said I would repair Foxy for him at home, and I put Foxy into my bag. Andy kept calling after me, "Foxy sad!" I kept repeating that I would repair him. The next day, I brought the repaired Foxy to school, and Andy grabbed him and exclaimed, "That's better!" which made everyone smile.

CHAPTER 18

ROSIE

During the last term with Annie, she was so much improved that I wasn't needed at all for her. She was even starting to eat her lunch in the dining hall with the other children on Fridays (and managing it very well) I was able to help with other children as well as her.

I noticed one day that Rosie, a very able girl who was right at the top of the class academically with the standard of her writing and reading, was beginning to struggle with her handwriting practice. She was also struggling with her numeracy in the mornings and was having catch-up sessions for that each day. It was hard to put my finger on what the problem was, since her writing was so beautifully neat and she quickly completed each handwriting practice lesson, but there were two other girls equally fast who were pulling away speed-wise, and Rosie was getting upset and making silly mistakes, such as missing whole lines, in her haste to keep up with them. She would come back from her catch-up numeracy session and then rush to finish her handwriting, but she would always be third in line after the other two girls to show the teacher her finished work. It was hard for me to see how upset and frustrated she was becoming, though I really couldn't see why.

I was already a little reticent to talk much to her since her mum was a lunchtime supervisor who often accompanied us on trips out and she and I had had words before. If I ever spoke to Rosie about her behaviour in the playground (she was often very mean and spiteful towards Annie and played another friend called Ellie and Annie against each other whenever she could), when her mum found out, she would come and tell me not to talk to Rosie!

During one memorable occasion on a trip around Hill Close Gardens, a little Victorian allotment area adjacent to the school, Annie had picked up a little polystyrene egg she had found on the ground. (It was the Easter bonnet parade, and lots of children had these eggs on their hats.) It was a very pretty little egg, and it was impossible to tell which hat it had fallen off, so Annie had asked if she could have it and I, in a moment of madness (I should have realised it would cause trouble!) said she could. Rosie was very jealous and was hoping to find one herself. When it came time to walk back to school, Rosie decided to be Annie's partner instead of Ellie's, which Annie was pleased about, but it upset Ellie, so I became Ellie's partner instead to calm her down. Annie and Rosie walked together just in front of us.

Rosie asked to see the egg, and she was shown it, but then she snatched it and called her mum over and asked her to put it in her bag. Annie was very annoyed, and I asked Rosie's mum to give the egg back to Annie, since it was she who had found it. Rosie's mum was furious with me, saying that Annie had stolen it anyway and how dare I call her Rosie a thief!

One day in class, I was happy that both Annie and Ellie were happily doing their handwriting practice, and I wandered around to see who else I could help. Rosie was hunched over her book, writing frantically, and she was flushed with effort. She kept looking up to see how far the other two girls had got and then swishing her lovely red hair around her like a curtain to cover her book and writing again. I got a little closer to try to see how she was writing, and I complimented her on her lovely neat work. She began to show me how she wrote, and I realised what the problem was immediately! Each letter was perfectly formed, with the little flick on the end needed to join it to the next letter, but each letter was being formed individually; she was then taking her pencil off the page, looking at the next letter to copy, and then carefully joining it on correctly. The writing itself was completely flawless and so neat, but she wasn't doing it cursively;

she wasn't actually writing with the letters joined up, although the finished work looked as though she was!

I showed her how to look at each word as a whole instead of as a series of letters, and I told her not to take her pencil off the page until she got to either a letter which couldn't be joined properly or the end of the word. She had a go and made a few mistakes but kept trying. By the end of the lesson, she had managed it perfectly, but she was at the end of the line since it had taken so long. She was disappointed at how long it had taken, but after that she got faster and faster and was eventually the first to finish, and it was all done cursively; she was delighted with herself!

She said to me a few days later that she hadn't realised that that was how she should have been doing it. I thought back and I realised that at the start of each handwriting lesson, she had regularly been going out to have a session with another teaching assistant (who did catch-up sessions for those falling behind with numeracy and other subjects), and she therefore was missing the carpet time when the teacher was showing the children how to join each batch of letters up properly, and so she was coming in and rushing to copy down the handwriting sheet into her book so she would be able to go out to play with the others. It was so simple, but we had all missed it! When I spoke to the teacher about it, she was very surprised as she hadn't noticed, Rosie's work was always completed quickly and neatly, she hadn't checked to see how she was doing it!

I had been worried that I had overstepped the mark and offered help to a child who seemingly didn't need it, and I was very pleased to have been able to help Rosie, even though she was an able child who seemed not to need any help.

I had suggested to Nigel at the start of my new job at Charles's old school that we put my salary aside and that I use it to pay for our summer holiday that year, and he had agreed, and so Charles and I had pored over brochures, and we had decided to go to Egypt. This we did, and we had a magical eleven days away. We thoroughly enjoyed ourselves, and I was delighted to be able to pay for all of it myself! We visited Cairo, the pyramids of Giza, and the Egyptian Museum; travelled through the three deserts (Black, White, and Great), camping each night; and then went to Luxor and Hurgarda, where we went snorkelling in the Red Sea for one magical afternoon.

I had completed my first year and had managed to help Annie, Andy, Ellie, and Rosie in a big way, so I was feeling confident about my next challenge—the following school year with another child.

CHAPTER 19

LILY

During the last few weeks of the term, I had been going with the SENCO to a school in Dudley to meet a little girl called Lily. It was quite a long drive and offered a chance to talk about things other than the immediate child we were dealing with. I was able to tell her all about my own schooling and going to a special school for maladjusted girls. She was so surprised and said she could not tell that I had had such problems myself. I said I felt that was why I was able to understand these children better than others; I had been just like them in my own youth.

Lily, the child we were visiting, was going to transfer to our school in the new school year, and we were going to meet her and her teaching assistants at her current school in Dudley. We went a couple of times, seeing her in her classroom and talking to the staff about her. She was a complex child—an 8-year-old who had been fostered since the age of two in lots of families, all of whom had found her too much to cope with.

She had been with her current foster family since October of the previous year, so she had been with them for about ten months. She now lived in the town I lived in with her new foster mum and her own son, a 5-year-old who was also starting at our school in September.

Lily was, at that time, travelling to school in Dudley every day from home by taxi, a forty-five-minute ride there and back, and was looking forward to being able to walk to school next term. She had only ever been to that school in Dudley, and it was therefore the only constant thing in her life, so it was a huge step for her to be leaving her school. We were hoping to make it an easy step for her, going to see her as often as we could and getting to know her so that at least we two would be familiar to her. We were learning all about her difficulties so we could make it a smooth transition for her.

We learned that Lily was struggling with relationships, distrusting adults, and not liking her peers. She was close to the older girls at her school, valuing their friendship above all others. She was constantly trying to upset people, particularly at home. We were told she had confessed at school one morning to her teaching assistant that she had killed her guinea pig before school by squeezing it to death and that she had then put it back into its cage, dead. The teaching assistant had hardly believed that she could do such a thing, but the next day she was informed by Lily's foster mum that it was indeed mysteriously dead and that it had been buried in the garden. The teaching assistant hadn't dared to phone and talk to her about Lily's confession that time, but the next time Lily confessed something—that she had left urine and faeces in the teapot at home—she had phoned to let her know and found that, indeed, she had.

Another day, Lily flooded the whole of the toilet block at school by stuffing all the paper into all the toilets and flushing them one by one. She was now saying she was afraid of flooding toilets.

The taxi journeys were a huge problem. Lily was enjoying them, but that was partly because she was being given a large bag of sweets to eat on the way there and back, so she was eating them all on the way and arriving at school really hyped up. The teaching assistants had taken to removing the sweets as soon as her taxi arrived, which was sending Lily into a rage each morning, and her mum wouldn't stop giving them to her; the school felt maybe it was because she felt guilty for making Lily go so far each day on her own. In every other way, Lily's mum seemed so sensible and switched on, so it seemed a strange thing to do, which was almost guaranteed to sabotage any chance of a good day at school for Lily.

The school had discovered early on that if they made Lily tidy up any mess she made at school, or if they told her mum about any sanctions, such as missing playtimes or treats at school, then her mum would get very cross with them. She didn't believe in making Lily pay for anything she'd done and didn't like to hear of any such sanctions. She used only positive behaviour to make Lily behave well for her, never anything negative.

Lily was also plagued with head lice. Possessing a beautiful head of bright red hair, she always stood out in a crowd, but she also stood out because she was always scratching, and her mum said that getting rid of head lice wasn't a priority for her, so she didn't deal with that all at all, which upset Lily's teachers and peers alike. It must have been horrible for Lily too!

In between a few disturbing incidences, Lily was generally OK and quite happy, although if she was upset, she would fly into a terrible temper and destroy displays and bookshelves at school.

She spent a lot of the time, we were told—and certainly it was true when I was with her observing her in the classroom at her school in Dudley—underneath the table, messing with water bottles, and going to the toilet, where she would refuse to come out of the cubicle again. She wasn't getting any work done, although she was very capable. She read well (albeit never reading aloud to anyone, even her mum) and understood what she had read, and her handwriting was perfectly acceptable. She was struggling with numeracy and not attempting any in her lessons.

She was always very pleased to see me on my visits to Dudley, insisting on hugging me and wanting my arm around her shoulders. I felt that we would be OK, and I was looking forward to having her start with us the next term, where she was to be in year four. First, though, we had the six-week summer holiday to enjoy, and we were all looking forward to this. We were off to Egypt!

The teaching assistant in reception said she was going to be looking after Lily and her brother during their summer holidays at home, as her foster mum thought it would be really helpful for Lily to have someone she knew well in school next year. Her foster mum said she had been thinking of sending her to a country village school in the meantime but had subsequently decided to leave her where she was for another year, and then to find a school that they could walk to from home instead.

CHAPTER 20

THE START OF THE SCHOOL YEAR

Nigel had a lot of health problems in the months that followed. He had been receiving treatment for precancerous cells on the back of his neck and was prone to frequent stomach upsets. We went to many doctors' appointment on Monday mornings and Friday afternoons, to fit in with his work, and he continued to commute to Portsmouth each week.

I started back at school in September 2008, and everyone was very happy, getting to know their old friends again as well as new classmates, their new teachers, and their classrooms, and talking about their holidays. Reception's teaching assistant said she had indeed worked with Lily most days during the long summer break and had even gone on holiday with Lily's family. Lily, she said, was delightful—a very happy child who liked to pretend to be a frog when she was happy but a tiger when she wasn't. She said it would be best not to engage in talking to the tiger if Lily changed into one, as that meant she was feeling stressed.

I began my normal routine of coming in each day as before, at 12.15 p.m., for Andy's lunch break. I was able to stay until he went into school for the afternoon now, but then I took over with Lily at 1.15 p.m., as they were both in the Juniors, instead of Annie at 1.00 p.m. as before, for afternoon lessons. To begin with, Lily was very popular, as she was so smiley and nice to everyone. She got on with her work each day with no bother at all, wanted to hug her new teacher whenever she could, and settled in beautifully. I was able to sit next to her each afternoon and help her along, but she didn't really need any help, and so I was able to keep an eye on Annie and Ellie too, as they were both in the same class as Lily.

Ellie seemed especially happy to be back at school. She was clean and well fed and enthusiastic about everything. Her writing and reading had improved beyond measure, too. On the first day, she told me she was being collected by her new parents, as she was now living with a foster family. I learned that all four of the young siblings were still together and were staying with these foster parents. Over the holidays, social services had swung into action and removed them from their neglectful mother. I can't begin to express how wonderful it was to see those children flourish and blossom over the next few weeks. Annie, too, was very happy, working hard and even managing to eat her lunches in the dining hall every day instead of only on Fridays.

Then the bubble burst.

The teaching assistant who had Lily in the mornings began to report that Lily was spending hours in the toilets instead of in the classroom, was beginning to be rude to her, and was refusing to come in after playtimes in the mornings and at lunchtime too. In the afternoons, she also began to spend ages in the toilets and was trying to find ways to get out of school and into the playground whenever she could. Outside in the playground, she found that she could go underneath the safety fence, and she was soon climbing up the scaffolding and swinging on the bars at a dizzying height. Indeed, she had even gone up a ladder to the roof! She was pretending to be a tiger, and the scaffolding became her cage.

In the afternoon, she would often politely ask to go to the toilet, but then, having left the classroom, she would instead run to the hall and climb the PE apparatus bars, swinging from the very top and laughing at me, saying, "Ha ha, I tricked you!" This was very dangerous, and she did it over and over again.

Nothing I said made any difference. I tried to reason with her, but when in tiger mode Lily was impossible to talk to; she manipulated everything anyone said and was rude and spiteful. In the mornings, two members of staff had taken to sitting at either end of the bars in the hall so Lily couldn't climb up, but in the afternoons, I was on my own, and she went up day after day.

For a while I managed to distract her enough to keep her mostly in the classroom, and when she earned a treat for doing some work I did let her play a game or do some drawing, but always in the classroom so she didn't get chance to climb the bars if I could help it. If I slipped up and she managed to climb up but then came down from the bars, I would allow her to play with play dough in the classroom, but she soon got wise and started coming down only if the treat offered was good enough.

The secretary was asked by the head to keep some little jobs to offer to Lily if she would come down, such as counting out and distributing letters to the classes, and Lily always enjoyed doing that.

Lily refused, at first, to join in with PE on Tuesdays, which was a surprise, as we had been assured that she loved PE at her old school. She did enjoy swimming and, from the first day, had been coming with us to the pool each Monday afternoon on the coach. She also had a regular piano lesson each Monday afternoon, so that was the plan on Mondays; she had her piano lesson, went to the toilet quickly and sensibly, and then came with the class on the coach to the swimming pool.

She began to mess around in the pool after a couple of weeks of good behaviour, swimming her width as asked but then refusing to get out of the water, so keeping the whole class waiting. I took her to get changed early one week, so she missed the free play session at the end, which she was very annoyed about, but the next week she was as good as gold and got the play session too.

Then one Monday I came to find Lily, having delivered Andy to his afternoon helper, on the floor outside the classroom, with a sopping wet ink pad in her hand, daubing the walls and carpets, and trying to get her assistant's smart leather boots too. I spoke to her, telling her she would need to get all the ink off her hands before she could have her piano lesson, and she came with me to wash herself. Her other assistant went home, and I took over as usual. Lily couldn't get the ink off her hands, arms, and face, so I said she couldn't have her piano lesson in case she spoiled the piano keys. She tried to get it off again but couldn't, so I wouldn't even take her swimming, as she would not have been allowed into the pool looking like that, so we spent a quiet afternoon in the classroom drawing seashells instead.

I later learned, after she'd gone home, that she'd spent the morning messing with the science resources, spoiling coloured squares of felt and winding nylon thread around her legs and bouncing around as if she were Zebedee from *The Magic Roundabout*, with it all up her legs. When she had begun to wind it around her neck too, she had been restrained, and it had all been cut off. She had broken a magnifying glass and tried to snap all the glass thermometers too.

It hadn't been a good day, and it was capped by her mum being furious about Lily's lost piano lesson and swimming lesson. The head phoned her after school to explain just how much of the school's resources Lily had ruined that day, and Lily came into school the next morning with a letter of apology. After that it was as though Lily had decided to stop being good at all.

One day one of the girls in her class had a home-made tiger hand puppet which she had brought in for Friday's golden time, a free play session each week at the end of the afternoon on Fridays, which the children could earn for good behaviour all week. Of course, Lily liked the puppet and wanted to keep it, and so, instead, on the following Monday the other child brought in enough prepared pieces for Lily to make her own puppet.

It was a lovely gesture, so kind and friendly, but it backfired. Lily stuck the black stripes all over her own face and became a raging tiger all afternoon. Her behaviour was atrocious, and it carried on for quite a few days after that. Once we had managed to get rid of all the stripes, she carried on anyway, becoming more and more violent. We kept trying though.

One day in the head's office, where were increasingly having to take Lily to calm down, I mentioned how much she reminded me of Pippi Longstocking, a character in a book I had read as a girl. The head laughed and said she had made the exact same comment earlier that day! She looked at Amazon on her computer while we were all in her office, and she found the books, still available, and with delightful illustrations.

Lily was raging around the room, damaging files and displays, and she even kicked the computer to try to get our attention. The head was extremely annoyed with her, but she began to read the first chapter aloud to Lily, and we were both surprised to hear that Pippi was an orphan whose parents had died and who lived on her own. Neither of us remembered that bit!

Although we both felt that it may have been a huge mistake to bring that subject up with Lily, I thought afterwards that actually it might even help Lily, and that to get to know Pippi, who had so much in common with Lily, might even be useful for her. Lily was interested, and despite herself she stopped and listened, and I mentioned the books to her mum on the playground at the end of the day. She had never even heard of Pippi (which really made me feel old) but said she would try to get some for Lily to read.

On the Saturday of that week, I was in town and picked up a leaflet about a festival that was happening in a couple of weeks' time that would be celebrating writing in all forms. I was delighted to see that the library was offering to host a Pippi Longstocking party! I showed the leaflet to Lily's mum at school, but she was way ahead of me and had already booked. She said that the whole family were going as a celebration of Lily's first anniversary of living with them. Of course, Lily had a wonderful time and a brilliant anniversary weekend full of celebrations and parties.

I had been wondering if the looming anniversary itself was maybe bothering her at school. Something certainly was anyway. She had been quite agitated on the thirtieth of September and had been asking over and over, "Is it the last day?" As it was a Tuesday, I didn't understand what she was asking at first, but then the penny dropped and I realised she thought that October, being the first anniversary, might bring more rejection for her.

We really paid for her wonderful weekend at school the next week. Her mum was cheerful about it, she called it "displaced emotion" and wasn't at all surprised. The following weekend was a nightmare for her mum, however. Lily, probably expecting more festivities, had played her up from morning to night all weekend, and she was exhausted. She said, "I give up!" shaking her head and looking very pale, but when I looked at her sharply, she pulled herself together and said she was joking, of course.

The next week was reasonable, and Lily actually earned enough tokens to swap them for a ballet lesson on Friday afternoon, The SENCO was happy to spend a session with Lily in the hall, showing her some ballet steps, and Lily loved it.

The next Monday, Lily did come swimming with us OK, but she spent the whole time when the children were changing in the changing rooms talking to me about what would happen if her new mummy died, asking whether she would she live in an orphanage and who would look after her. She wouldn't even leave the small room to go to the pool and was very upset, so I was quite concerned, and I wondered what had been said at home in the heat of the moment. Lily's teacher and I decided to keep an eye on what Lily was worrying about and not mention to her mum what she had said to me.

The next afternoon, the Tuesday, was very good, with Lily even joining in with PE for the first time, which she enjoyed right up until the last fifteen minutes of the day. It was as though had Lily suddenly realised she'd forgotten to be naughty, so she zipped up the bars at the end of PE at 3.00 p.m. and refused to come down.

The class had been a bit upset anyway, as one of the girls had suddenly thrown up in the hall during PE, and Lily had wanted to inspect the vomit closely, loving the smell of the disinfectant brought by the caretaker to clean up for us and shadowing the girl who'd been sick, even following her to the toilets to wash her face.

She told me she had threadworms that day too and was scratching at her bottom most unpleasantly. When she did come down from the bars, she began to grab at my top and sleeves, twisting the material and trying to rip it. She scratched at my face and hands too, and it was all I could do to get her back to the classroom in one piece myself. The class had already changed back into their uniforms and were ready to go home. Lily was still in her PE kit. I encouraged her to get dressed while the other children lined up at the door and told her that her mum and brother would be wondering where she was.

As the children and teacher left the class to go home, Lily flew into a rage without warning and raced around the classroom, wrecking displays and knocking books to the floor. She ran to the table where the pencils and scissors were kept, grabbed a handful of scissors, and started throwing them at me like arrows. I quickly got out of the room and closed the door, trapping her inside but still being able to see her through the glass.

It was lucky that it was a Tuesday, as the SENCO was in school that day; I sent a messenger to see if they could find her for me. Then another parent came to the class with her own daughter to fetch something that she'd forgotten, so I took my chance and shot up to the office while they were with Lily (as she was suddenly calm and pleased to see them) to see if I could find anyone to help me. The SENCO came back with me and tried to sort Lily out, but she reverted to being a tiger in seconds. She danced around behind the SENCO, holding the scissors, and looking at me and gesticulating that she was going to cut my hair with them, so I kept well away. The other mum went out again and asked Lily's mum to come and get her, which she did, and Lily was suddenly smiley and calm again. I left them to it!

The next day followed the same pattern. Lily brought me a note to apologise, but she had written "Dear Mrs Patrick, I apologise for being ever so naughty and I won't ever ever, ever do it again (from the student who no longer loves you)". Her mum thought it was sincere, but Lily just thought it was funny. She came into class after lunch, although she went up the bars in the hall briefly first, but she came down with the promise of a magazine I had brought in for her to look at. The magazine was all about space and had a lovely 3D poster with special 3D glasses to look at it with, and the magazine itself was full of 3D pictures too. We had been making planets with the play dough during the previous few sessions in class and playing hide-and-seek with our Pluto, so I thought it might interest her. There was also an article on hiccups, which we had been talking about the day before, and on the back of the 3D space poster was the best bit for Lily—another poster, this time a picture of a family of koalas, her mum's favourite animal.

At 3.10 p.m., five minutes before home time, having been fine all afternoon looking at the magazine and listening to the lesson, she suddenly ran out of the classroom, and I found her in the girls' toilets, where she had climbed onto the basins and was swinging from the water pipes on the ceiling. She was kicking out at me and spitting at me, and so I kept out of range and sent another child, who had, luckily for me, arrived in the toilets too, to get the head for me. Lily came down eventually before she arrived, and she ran upstairs again into the hall. The head came through to the hall just in time, and we blocked the bottom of the bars (to an amusing "Oh, bother!" from Lily), but she still managed to get a foot rubber off a PE table and put it in her mouth, and she ran around laughing at us. Her mum came into the hall looking for Lily just then, and Lily defied her too.

I looked after her brother while the head and her mum calmed Lily down, and Lily and her mum and brother went off in a hurry, as they had an appointment with the dentist. Her mum warned Lily that if they got to the dentist in time for their appointment, they would have a nice evening; otherwise, they would not. I was late going home again, and exhausted. I could see a pattern developing but just didn't know how to help.

The next day at school was much better, although the previous evening at home had been fraught, and the dental appointment missed. Lily had a good ICT lesson; since she was already in the ICT suite after lunch, and I didn't have to get her there. She asked to go to the toilet when she had finished her work. I must have looked a bit dubious, but she hissed that she needed a poo, so I said, "OK, Lily, if I can trust you to come out of the toilets again afterwards?" and she said I could.

She was as good as her word and came out quickly, so I was pleased. We went back to the class afterwards instead of going back to the ICT suite, since it was almost home time anyway, and I figured that the class would be through very quickly and that letting Lily start on a computer again would be detrimental—I knew she wouldn't want to go home! In fact, the class were a long time coming back to the classroom, but Lily was calm and happy, playing with shells and play dough while we waited, and she went home on time.

The next day, a Friday, Andy was a little unsettled over his lunch break and didn't want to go outside, so I got a large wooden house out for him to play with inside instead. I carried it out of the year one classroom it was in, since it was just about time for the infants to come back into school after lunch and set it up in the wet area for him. While he played happily, suddenly there was a commotion and Ellie came in crying, holding her arm. As she was dealt with by the first aider, she tearfully told us all that Annie had attacked her, slapping and scratching her. Annie was sent for and brought inside by the head, and she left her with me while she went to find her assistant to have her. It was lucky I had the house out, as Annie and Andy played happily together with it. After a while, her assistant turned up, so she took Annie off. I needed to take Andy to his afternoon class too.

Lily's other support assistant came looking for me, as it was time for me to take Lily off her hands, so I quickly delivered Andy to his classroom and came straight back for Lily. The assistant said there was a lady in school who was observing Lily from a distance. She then handed me a damp blanket, which she said was Lily's "blankie" from home. She said Lily was in the computer suite and was refusing to leave to come to class for the afternoon.

Lily was indeed refusing to cooperate. She kept drawing on the computer and ignoring me, so I gave her a countdown of five down to zero. When I reached zero, I told her, I would turn off the computer for her. She just carried on, oblivious, so when I got to zero, I turned it off. She was cross and spat at me to go and get her blankie, as her other support assistant had taken it from her. I said that I had it, showed her, and told her she could have it back when she was in class, knowing full well that if I gave it to her now, she would just take it up the bars in the hall.

She was livid, made a grab for it, and got hold of a corner. And so began the tug of war. I had hold of the majority of the blanket; she had a corner, and she fought me for it. I kept repeating that she could have it in class, but she was in no mood to listen. She growled, kicked, bit and spat at me, but eventually realised I wasn't giving in. She then let go and ran off towards the classroom.

Of course, she was up the bars in the hall when I got there. She screamed at me to give her back her blankie "*now!*" I ignored her, and when the SENCO came through (thank goodness it was a Friday so she was in school!), we talked together about the toy that Lily had started to make in the classroom this morning—a red pom-pom which, once made, she was going to call Russ, and Russ was going to help her in literacy lessons, just as Fuzz, another furry toy from the SENCO room, had started to help her in numeracy.

Lily had earned enough tokens to "buy" this craft activity, and she did eventually come down again and back to class, and she carried on with her pom-pom making happily, even having to be reminded to take her blankie home at the end of the afternoon!

It being a Friday, the class then had golden time at 2.45 p.m., and Lily joined in enthusiastically as usual, having the free time even though she didn't deserve it at all. The SENCO and I had talked about giving Lily work to do from earlier in the day at golden time instead, but today didn't feel like the day to try it! I can just imagine how Lily would have reacted if I had tried that!

At 3.05 p.m. we had a visitor to the class—a support assistant who had been with us the previous year and was a very popular TA with the children at the school. The class surrounded her with whoops of delight (including Lily, who had never even met her before), and just before home time, Lily suddenly said she was going to the toilets, so I went with her.

She went to the toilet but refused to leave the room afterwards, climbing up again onto the basins and trying to reach the water pipes again. I could see that she would be out of reach in a second, and I decided to stop her whilst I could get in her way. I got close enough so she couldn't kick me, and peeled her fingers off the pipes, turned her around and marched her out and up the stairs as quickly as I could. She was so surprised she didn't try to fight!

When we got to the top of the stairs, however, she climbed onto the handrail by the slope and spat at me most unpleasantly. I told her that we don't spit at friends or people we like, or anyone else come to that, and asked her to stop. She didn't stop, but neither did she retort that I *wasn't* a friend, as I expected her to. I knew I had put myself in a silly position, just asking for trouble, but she didn't take the advantage that time.

She got down after a while and danced into the hall, grabbing at my top and trying to rip it, and scratching at my hands and face. If I faced her, I was spat at and scratched, and if I turned my back, I was pulled at and kicked. I wasn't very happy with the situation, but it was hard to get her to stop. Somehow I got back to the class in time to see the class lining up to go home, and Lily went into the classroom and started destroying the bookshelves again. As the children (and teacher) left, she began to hurl books at me Frisbee style, so I went out of the room and shut the door.

Lily threw herself at the door in rage and then destroyed a new display next to the door of a tree with green leaves on it and with orange leaves at the base. The children had been writing on the green leaves things they would take with them if they were leaving to go to an "ideal" school, and on the orange leaves, strewn around as though they had fallen off in autumn, were things they would leave behind. She chewed up some of the leaves and tried to spit them through the door lock at me.

Her mum came to find us just then and asked me not to open the door but to tell her what had been going on while Lily couldn't hear us, and Lily, still at large in the classroom, began pulling out drawers and spoiling other children's things. I explained carefully, and she listened gravely.

I gratefully left Lily to her mum as soon as she was ready to go in and get her, and I went to get myself ready to go home. I was still in the staff room, talking to Lily's class teacher, the head, and the observing lady about what had happened today, when a tap on the door told us that Lily was outside the door. She had a challenging expression on her face as she handed me a letter she had just written to one of the children (whose drawer she had just destroyed), and in it she said that the child had been calling her names and making her cry at playtime. Lily's mum was right behind her, saying that *this* was *obviously* the reason that Lily had been so upset, and crossly asking why we hadn't done *anything* about it. Since it was the first any of us had heard of such an incident, and as Lily was looking uncomfortable and saying that she must have "forgotten" to tell anyone, we really didn't believe it and put it down to Lily's craftiness and ability to hoodwink her mum.

This was the last day of the first half term with Lily, so we were all glad to leave and have a decent break! Lily had said she was going to Devon to the beach, but I was happy just to be at home and not have to do anything much.

We had a lovely holiday, but in no time at all it was time to go back to school.

CHAPTER 21

STARTINGBACKAFTERHALFTERM

Lily's week didn't start well. On the Monday morning, she kicked her teacher and threw a ball of play dough so hard that she hurt her other support assistant's eye. The afternoon with me, however, was fine. She enjoyed her piano lesson and went swimming like an angel, doing very well and even being asked to show the class her backstroke without armbands, so she was delighted with herself.

Tuesday was similar, although the class had had a supply teacher in the morning and he had been kicked and spat at, and Lily had found a sewing needle which she had been picking her teeth with.

The afternoon with me started OK. Lily was in class and sort of on task for a while, but she soon got fidgety. She wanted to count her tokens to see if she had enough to swap for a cooking session with her other support assistant. She needed seventy-two, she said, and she counted up and found that she had seventy-one. She was beside herself with excitement and wanted to go and tell the SENCO that she had only one to go. When we checked her treats sheet, we found that she needed seventy-five, in fact, so she really had to get another four, which was well within her reach if she stayed in class.

She couldn't contain herself, though, and ran to see the SENCO anyway. She was turned away, as the SENCO had the observing lady back again and was talking with her. Lily went back to class with me happily enough, and we played with play dough while she listened to the lesson about rainforests. It wasn't long before she decided to mess around instead, though, and before she could earn any more of the treasured tokens, she nipped out of the class and into the science resource room.

She tried to get at the drawer with the needles in it, but it had (mysteriously!) been moved higher up the shelving unit so she couldn't reach it. She found a piece of old ceiling tile somewhere, from where the roof was still being repaired and retiled, and she started to snap it into pieces and make a horrible chalky mess on the carpet. As it was 2.45 p.m., I suggested that we go to the computer room for the last bit of the afternoon, and she agreed readily. She was calm and happy in the computer suite, but she was still hanging on to the ceiling tile, and she began to chew on it and eat it. At 3.10 p.m., though, she came with me back to the class and began to get ready to go home.

I knew that the next day was going to be different for her, as I was going on a training course with her other support assistant and the SENCO in the afternoon. I had already told Andy who was going to look after him so that he would know what to expect. I mentioned it to Lily as well and told her who would be with her in the afternoon instead of me.

Lily, ready to go home, walked towards the steps to go outside and meet her mum and brother, but she suddenly ran into the hall instead and began climbing the bars again. She chewed more ceiling tile and started spitting the resulting goo out into the hall, all over the other children who had begun congregating for an after-school club in the hall. I tried to get the children to ignore her, but they were appalled at her behaviour and began to shout at her and tell her to get down and stop it, which she didn't.

Eventually her mum came to find us, but Lily wouldn't get down for her either. Her mum almost burst into tears; she was so tired and drawn, and she looked at me and said, "What do I do? I can't go up there after her." I said that we deal with this every day, and the only way is to distract her somehow. I offered to go and get a toy from the SENCO office, but she suddenly remembered that she had her camera in her bag and said she would show me the holiday video of their trip to Devon.

Of course, Lily was down in a heartbeat! When we had looked at it together, they went off home happily enough, and I went back to the class to tidy the mess we had left in there as usual.

The SENCO had the lady with her who had been watching Lily the other day, and they hailed me as I passed the office and wanted to know how I had managed today. The lady was very complimentary about how I had coped with the bits she had seen of our difficult afternoon, but she suggested that next time I had to be out of school for a planned training or something, I should perhaps give Lily a transition item for her to look after for me to prove that I was going to come back. She agreed it was right for me to have told Lily that I wouldn't be there the next day, but she thought an item like that might have helped. I hadn't thought about it like that, and we all agreed that maybe I had better get something to bring in each day so I would be better prepared the next time.

The next day at the training afternoon was brilliant. The child psychologist who was leading it showed us that different types of trauma will often present in particular types of behaviour. If you know the traumas experienced, she explained, then it is easier to see why a child behaves as he or she does, but if you don't know what the child has been through and are simply dealing with day to day behaviour, sometimes you can see a pattern and work backwards to understand what the child may have experienced.

One of the types of behaviour she was explaining about was very like Lily's, and that therefore pointed to Lily feeling ashamed of herself. An overwhelming shame, which is hard to get rid of, was manifesting itself, and obviously each episode of appalling behaviour was only adding to the shame she was feeling.

We learned that the triangle-shaped ladder of support we need to offer starts with the largest rung, the bottom one, which is to ensure that the child feels safe and secure in their environment at school. The next rung up is slightly smaller and deals with relationships with people around the child. Then comes fitting in and doing as is expected of them, and at the very top, the smallest rung, is counselling and talking about feelings. We learned that there was absolutely no point in trying to analyse things with Lily at this stage, since we were still on the bottom rung, and that trying to do so would make things worse for her. First up was making her feel safe and secure.

On Thursday I arrived early at work, and Lynne drew me into her office to talk to me. I told her how helpful the training had been and all about how I now thought Lily's problems stemmed from shame, and she said she wished she could have come too. Lily had broken more resources that morning (a globe, from which she had ripped the map paper and eaten, and then she had smashed the plastic globe itself for good measure). She also said that she was very worried since an OFSTED inspection was overdue and that she didn't want Lily to have another bad session with the inspectors observing. I said that as long as we all dealt with it correctly, it might be a good thing for them to see, but she was doubtful. She asked me to make sure I had lots of distractions up my sleeve next week, because she expected the call to come on Monday or Tuesday of that week.

I had a good afternoon with Lily that day, since I was now concentrating on making sure she felt safe and secure instead of insisting she did the set work. The class were not in the computer room for a change (which they usually were on a Thursday afternoon), so as Lily *was* there, I allowed her to stay there instead of insisting she went to the classroom, as I normally would have in those circumstances. I knew that her class were in the classroom, learning all about tree diagrams in preparation for their computer lesson the next week, so as Lily played, I made a few of those types of diagrams to show her. She wasn't very interested and even snarled that if that was what *they* were going to do for the next week, then *she* wasn't going to take part in the lesson.

We progressed towards the classroom when she got tired of playing on the computer, but she went straight past it, through to the science resource room, which was fascinating for Lily with all the boxes of interesting stuff in there. We didn't get out what she wanted (a thimble to play hunt the thimble), because last time we did that it was great fun, but at the end she refused to stop playing, and when I insisted, she turned into a tiger, hissed at me, and put the thimble in her mouth! It was only one of those orange rubber ones with little knobs all over it that secretaries use to turn pages, but it still could have choked her.

She helpfully informed me today that there was a little gold one that we could use instead, but I stuck to my guns and said no. She was very annoyed that they were out of her reach (funny that!) and that I wouldn't get them down for her, but I suggested something else we could do, and after a while we got some cooking weights out and a small pair of old-fashioned scales instead, and she played with that. I tried to keep it educational by talking about comparing weights, etc., and it was still fun.

I noticed rather quickly that she was letting lots of wind out; it was getting very noticeable and unpleasantly smelly in that little area. I didn't want to embarrass her, but I remembered when I used to work at the girls' prep school in the nursery that we used to ask if anyone needed to go to the toilet if there was that kind of smell emanating from the children. So, I quietly said, "Lily, do you need to go to the toilet?" She said "No!" Then she looked at me sideways and asked why I had asked her that. I said, "Well, you are making quite a few smells, aren't you?" She looked aghast, and whispered back, "Oh, can you smell it?" and I said I could, as she was "whizzpopping" quite a lot!

She looked at me with a bemused expression on her face and said, "Whizzpopping? What on earth is that?" I asked her if she had heard of *The BFG* by Roald Dahl, since that is where the expression comes from, and I said that was what we called them in our house (which was a white lie, but it made it easy to talk about). She laughed and confided in me that in her house they used an even funnier word; she whispered, "We call them farts!" and went off into peals of laughter. Well, I hadn't laughed so much in a long time. We were both giggling, as it was so funny. She said she hadn't heard of Roald Dahl or *The BFG*, so I said I would try to get a copy to show her.

I then made my hands into two large pink spiders and started to role play with them, with one spider whizzpopping and the other making funny comments, and Lily (whose hands were filthy since she had spent the morning covering herself in black ink again) joined in, making her hands into two black spiders. She said her hands were the children and my hands were the parents.

She insisted that the children had to be "borned" (sic) from the mother spider and were called Whizzpop One and Whizzpop Two. At her insistence, the daddy spider had to watch the birth, and he had to say, "Oh, I can see the head coming out," and then the two baby spiders took it in turn to whizzpop. I am sure the classes and teachers around us could hear us laughing, but it was a wonderful session, and I didn't curtail it. I made the daddy spider suggest that the mummy spider open a few windows to clear the air in the house from all the whizzpops, and then Mummy Spider told Daddy Spider to take the children out to the park so she could get some fresh air.

Daddy Spider then helped the babies onto his back and took the babies to the park and put them on the see-saw (the scales we had played with before), and they see-sawed happily, whizzpopping whenever they got to the top of the see-saw. It was a wonderful session. Lily hadn't laughed like that with me since I had known her. We were both crying with laughter by home time. She happily helped me tidy up and went off home with no trouble that day.

The next day, a Friday, Andy was unwell, but he didn't get to go home, because no one was in. Although the secretary phoned home three times, it was to no avail. He was very quiet all lunchtime and seemed to be sad and kept saying "Andy poorly! Andy want Ann (his mum)." It was so sad, but there was nothing I could do about it.

That afternoon, I made no attempt at getting Lily into the classroom; we just had fun. When she came through the foyer after lunch, after I had dropped Andy off in his classroom and was coming to find her, she leapt up at me and threw herself into my arms, so I had no choice but to catch her. She refused to let go, so I sank backwards onto a soft chair by the bookshelves, and she remained on my lap for a close cuddle for quite a few minutes.

She said that my jumper was nice and soft, and that I smelled nice. She then told me that it just wasn't fair that she was having to forgo her *Beano* comic this week because of that stupid globe, which she had accidently (!) broken. After a while, she slid off and picked up a book from the shelf—an Oxford Reading Tree book, stage 8, which was a long story about "Kipper the super dog" and was great. She climbed back onto my lap and really relaxed into the story. The head walked past and said with feeling, "Oh, that looks lovely; I bet you are both enjoying that!" which we were. We got through about six books before Lily decided she wanted to do something else.

She had a little toy with her that day—a small rat with a long tail that her mum had given her, called "Grey". Grey crawled all over me and through my hair and over my face while we read the stories together, but I didn't mind.

Lily told me that she had earned enough tokens for her cooking session, so we talked about what she would like to cook, and she decided on flapjacks. I said we could cook on Tuesday afternoon (since Monday afternoon would be busy with her piano lesson and swimming as usual), and she was happy with that. We then went down to the computer room, which she said she would prefer to do rather than go to her class to join in with golden time that week, and it was fine. She went home on time again, quite happy.

I spoke to the SENCO when she'd gone, to see if it was OK for me to find a copy of *The BFG* to read to Lily the next week (mindful of the looming OFSTED inspection and the need to distract Lily), and she said she had a copy for me to borrow, which she would bring on Tuesday when she came to work. She also said she had a good recipe for flapjacks and a baking tray I could use.

We talked about our afternoon, and she was delighted that things were settling nicely again, and that Lily was so much less aggressive at the moment. My only gut-churning moment was when she said she thought maybe she'd better not tell me where Grey had been all morning. I said, "Oh no, *not* down the loo?" and she laughed and said, "Oh no, you're all right, only down Lily's knickers!" Well, that really brought me back down to earth with a bump, and I shot off home to have a shower! After that, the days just got better.

On Monday Lily was as usual delighted to see me when I arrived in school, and I was able to spend an extra hour with Lily alongside her other support assistant because Andy was off sick with a chest infection. I was able to smooth the transition between her other support assistant's care and mine by reading a book with Lily (in our "cuddle chair", as she now called it, in the foyer) at 1.00 p.m. so that her other support assistant was able to leave at 1.15 p.m. Lily was happy to go to her piano lesson on time, and also to go swimming, even though she was again covered in ink from the morning; she was doing this a lot whenever she got hold of something that would colour her skin. We were told by the educational psychologist that it was a symptom of Lily wanting to be someone else and not herself—that is, it was a form of disguise. She had found and grabbed a spent (but alas not quite!) red ink cartridge from the printer and had dotted her face all over to make herself look as if she had chicken pox. She had rubbed it over her lips like lipstick too and looked like a clown. She had washed most of it off by the time I saw her, so I allowed her to go swimming in the hope that it would simply wash off in the water, and it wasn't so noticeable that anyone there was likely to complain—not like the time she had done it with black ink.

The swimming lesson went well; all the ink came off, and so did Lily's armbands, permanently, as she was much improved. The teacher was very pleased with her.

The next afternoon was as successful, and as Andy didn't come in all week, I had lots of extra time with Lily over lunchtimes. I had brought in all that I needed for her cooking session, and we made some delicious flapjacks together. Lily wanted to give them out all over the school (the SENCO thought that this was to apologise for her behaviour and make people like her again), so we bagged up twenty-three little pieces for the children in her class and a few extra for select members of staff. Lily took what was left home with her to share with her mum and brother.

The rest of the week, at least the afternoons with me, passed calmly and happily. Lily remained settled and didn't climb the PE bars at all that week, which was lovely, and she enjoyed lots of closeness with me, reading or playing games. Her other support assistant began to report that mornings were getting better too, and Lily was even doing literacy lessons by choice, and doing them well.

Wednesday and Thursday passed in the same vein, and I saw no reason why things would change. But change they did—not as far as Lily was concerned, but for me. I had a bipolar episode that stole up on me so slowly I didn't recognise it at first.

I had lots of energy. I was spending my mornings and evening frantically cleaning the house thoroughly, and it helped me deal with Lily too; I was able to think quickly and keep one step ahead of her for a change. She began to look sideways crossly at me and tell me I was "too clever" and "too good" at the guessing games we were playing. We played games to use up her surplus energy—hockey in the hall, skipping in the playground—and I was able to think about what I needed to be saying to people about her so that they could help too. The SENCO was delighted, and so was the head. It seemed that things were looking up for Lily's immediate future.

CHAPTER 22

BIPOLAR AGAIN

I noticed I had lost two pounds in weight without trying to and was pleased at the side effect of all the cleaning.

On Friday morning, I was going to have coffee with my niece and her seven-week-old son, but she phoned me on the Thursday evening to cancel, saying that she had scalded her hand making herself coffee and had had to go to hospital to have it checked and dressed. She was going back to hospital in the morning so wouldn't be in for our coffee. I asked her how she was getting there, knowing that her boyfriend would be at work, and she said, "Oh, I don't know; I might take a bus, or else I'll walk".

I offered to take her myself so that we could still meet as we'd wanted to and we could have our coffee afterwards, and she accepted my offer with pleasure. Her appointment was for 10.10 a.m., so I collected her at 9.50 a.m. She was seen quickly by the nurses, who said that her scald was completely gone, but they were concerned for the baby, who had had a rash the day before, and the doctor wanted to see him while they were there.

We had to wait for ages for him to be seen, and we were still sitting there at 11.00 a.m., so I said I would phone the school secretary to say I couldn't make it that day rather than have to rush and be late or leave them on their own, which I then did. She said it was fine and that she would let the head know, and that I was not to worry, as they would sort something out for Lily and Andy.

The baby was eventually seen, and they had to stay in the hospital with him for even longer, as the doctor wanted another specialist doctor to come and have a look, thinking maybe he had measles. My niece was quite upset, the baby was crying, and her mum was nowhere to be seen; she had been texting her all morning, asking her to come and stay with her so I could get off to work, but she didn't reply. She said she was so pleased I was there, so I felt that I couldn't go and leave her.

The head phoned me on my mobile phone; she was extremely annoyed that I wasn't coming into school; she said that Lily was completely hyper and that they needed me there. I felt that family had to come first, and I told her so, and I didn't leave them. Thinking back, I could easily have done so, but in my heightened state I was feeling that they needed me more, and anyway, I was enjoying being with her and the baby, so I stayed where I was. We were able to leave the hospital at about 2.30 p.m., and I took them home.

Nigel was home early that day; he arrived home at about 3.00 p.m., so we had a quick cup of tea and took ourselves off to Charles's school, where we had an appointment with *his* SENCO. I was concerned that Charles had recently stopped using his AlphaSmart, as he said his writing was now neat enough. Of course, no one else could read it still, and I was aware that he had his first GCSE exam (science) looming in January.

We then had a busy weekend at home as a family, although I wasn't feeling at all well. I was starting a cold; I had a cold sore on my lip, which hurt, and I got very tired. On the Monday, I awoke with a very sore throat and no voice, so I phoned in sick to work. I spent the day cleaning the house when I was supposed to be resting, and although I had a lie-down after lunch, I couldn't sleep. Charles came home after school, and we went out to buy something he needed. I cooked tea and then spent the evening sorting out recipes, not realising quite how hyper I was myself. I didn't go out in the evening, even though we were supposed to be going to singing rehearsals for a musical drama we were going to be performing at church, as my throat was too sore, and Charles decided he didn't want to go without me.

On the Tuesday I slept late, but Charles got up as usual and brought me a cup of tea when he'd finished his paper round. After he'd gone to school, I had my breakfast, had a shower, and began to clean the bathroom. At 1.30 p.m., I finished the deep clean I had started after breakfast and started looking around for something else to clean!

I realised how ridiculous it all was when I noticed my poor, sore hands after all the cleaning, and the smell of bleach permeating the house. I phoned my consultant psychiatrist and spoke to his secretary, who listened and booked me in for an appointment the following morning.

That evening, I was supposed to be at a social gathering with my Bible study group—a meal out at a local Chinese restaurant which I had been looking forward to—and I was picking up our minister's wife so she wouldn't have to go on her own. I didn't feel at all well though, so I had to cancel and ask someone else to take her, and someone else did.

I was feeling defeated, thinking that my bipolar had got me again and was going to ruin my career and stop me working for weeks until I felt better, as it had once before when Charles was in year seven and I had missed eight weeks of work, waiting until I felt better.

Then, after a while, I felt much calmer. I realised that if I just pulled myself back together, I could go to see my doctor, talk to him and see what he had to say, and still get to work on the Wednesday afterwards if he felt I was fit to go, especially as we had an important meeting arranged to sort out Lily's Individual Education Plan (IEP) at noon on the Wednesday.

On the Wednesday, I was very aware of the need to be at work for noon. I, of course, was also worrying that I might be late for work, but just as I was leaving for my appointment, the phone rang. It was the secretary from the office at school to say that the SENCO had asked her to call me to say that I wasn't needed that desperately; if I didn't feel able to go, then

I didn't need to, and she would take copious notes for me to have later. That was a relief, and I got myself off to my appointment in Kenilworth.

My appointment went very well, I managed to articulate all that I was feeling, and my doctor again decided to change my medication, this time to a new version of quetiapine, Seroquel XL, which was a slow-release version, meaning I could take twice as much, as it took longer to be absorbed, and it would work all day long instead of just overnight. He also said that it was reasonable for me to take the rest of the week off work.

I couldn't get the tablets that day, as they were so newly available, so that evening I planned to take an extra half a tablet of my usual medication instead, which would knock me out completely and would make me take much longer than usual to get going in the morning, but I wanted to increase the medication as soon as I could.

That afternoon, I popped into school after the children had left to see the head, to explain why I wasn't at work. The head was so cross and exploded, saying that if all I had was a sore throat (which she could hear, as I was very husky) then I should be pushing through it and coming into work. She complained that I had already had a lot of time off this term (which I wasn't so very aware of; I had had some time off with tonsillitis diagnosed by my GP, but it had been just four days, so I hadn't been able to get a sick note for her). I accepted that I had had the odd day off here and there as well, but the one she was particularly cross about was the Friday I had spent with my niece and the baby at hospital. She said that my work must always come first and that I should have left them to it and collected her later in the day after work.

I explained how awful I was feeling, how worried I was with Nigel's hospital visits and skin problems, and with Charles needing a new computer for school (since his AlphaSmart was no longer much use to him). I explained about being bipolar and about how I must respect the illness and make sure that my medication is effective, and that at the moment, although feeling physically better in myself, I was feeling very shaky and was about to try out a new medication—and that my doctor had said it was very reasonable for me to take the rest of the week off.

The head asked the SENCO to come through to her office, and I explained everything again, although the SENCO already knew about my bipolar disorder (from when we had been travelling to meet Lily in Dudley during the previous term). They both agreed that I *was* certainly the best person for this job, that I should take as long as I needed to recover, and that I should not worry about work! The head conceded that she always knew when I was in school, as everything stepped down a gear and everyone became calmer, to which she added, "And that *is* a compliment, Jenny!"

The next time we spoke, she admitted that she had had a letter explaining about my bipolar disorder from the occupational therapist when I applied for the position, but that she had filed it unread. She therefore had not realised that I would need time to recover from any episodes. She assured me that she had now read it and I was not to worry. Any time I needed off was fine, but I was to give her as much notice as possible.

CHAPTER 23

BACK AT WORK

On Monday, I went back to work as I had promised. Lily was hesitant at first, very suspicious of me and not keen to sit with me. Then she suddenly changed her mind and jumped onto me delightedly and wouldn't let me go! The call, I heard, had not come through for OFSTED, so we were OK for a while, and I just concentrated on Lily. We went swimming as usual, and Lily had a great lesson, but when she got into the shower afterwards, she suddenly changed personality again. She stopped looking at me, stopped talking to me, and just froze. I couldn't get anything out of her, and she ignored all instructions to go and get changed. In the end, the class left without us, and the head had to be asked to come and collect the two of us in her car instead.

She was not impressed with Lily but was very happy with me and didn't seem to blame me, which was a great relief! She explained that the very same thing had happened the week I was away, and that Lily had been warned not to do it again. She added that Lily was *not* going to be going swimming again, and that she would therefore miss out on being awarded the swimming badge the next week, which was the last session of swimming anyway.

The next day, being a Tuesday, the SENCO was in school, and I got there early so we could talk. The head came in and said she had just had the call and that our OFSTED inspection was going to be on Wednesday and

Thursday of that week. I wasn't worried. I had no intention of changing how I did things, even if everyone else went into a flat spin and suddenly made their classrooms and the wall displays newer and better.

The Wednesday went very well again in the afternoon, although I heard that the morning had been atrocious as far as Lily was concerned. I had had difficulty parking my car as usual in the school car park, as people had parked inconsiderately, as they often did, leaving the middle spaces empty to leave their own car able to be driven out again at some point in the afternoon without having to ask anyone else to move his or her car first. It was worse than usual though, and when I was asked to move my car to let Faith (the new morning teacher for the SEN children in her "Sparkle" classroom) out at 12.55 p.m., I commented that if people would only park better, then we could *all* get in properly, and she took it very personally. She said, "Well, I *always* park there; I have to leave at 1.00 p.m." She was so snooty, as though her time was more important than everyone else's, and I was annoyed too. Her parting comment was "That was the least of our troubles *today!*" I can only assume she was referring to the OFSTED inspection, which, as I have said before, should make *no* difference, in my opinion.

The Thursday went well as usual for me and Lily—with another bad morning though, unfortunately. I was irritated since I didn't actually see any inspectors on the two afternoons I was there when they were, which meant they had only seen Lily at her worst in the mornings and not when she was settled with me.

On Thursday after school, everyone heaved a huge sigh of relief when the inspectors left, and after the children had all gone home, all the teachers met in the staff room to discuss how things had gone. I didn't hear anything, good or bad, about the inspection, but I hoped it had gone well. One of the other teaching assistants spoke to me and said that I should ask the head how it had gone, as she had some inkling but wasn't allowed to talk about it publicly yet. I didn't get a chance, and weeks later I still didn't know how it went! Once the results finally came through, we were delighted to have got a wonderful report, with the special needs care specifically commended.

On the Friday there was an air of excitement around the school, as we were holding the Christmas fayre in the afternoon. Lily was distracted and excited like the others, and we spent a lot of the afternoon in the Special Educational Needs (SEN) room writing jokes on the whiteboard and playing with the soft toys in there. At 3.05 p.m., Lily's mum and brother came to collect her to go around the fayre together. Lily's mum asked me to stay with her, as she didn't feel able to manage both children on her own, and I said I would stay with her until 3.15 p.m., when I wanted to get off home. She was a bit annoyed and said that she wouldn't have finished with the fayre by then and wanted me to stay with her until she left!

At 3.15 p.m., she and the children had mostly done everything in the hall and were eating hot dogs, so I said I needed to go. I left them to it, and she was quite happy. I found, however, that I was blocked into the car park by a car I didn't recognise. So, I went back into the fayre, bought some items, and then sat with one of the teachers, chatting with her by her stall, to wait to the end of the sale, when hopefully whoever it was would move their car.

As I was talking to her, Faith came over to talk to her, and I phoned Charles on my mobile to explain why I was going to be late home. As I told him that I was boxed in in the car park, a look passed between them, and Faith began to look very smug. I asked them if they knew whose car it was in the car park, parked so inconsiderately, and of course it was Faith's *other* car. I asked her politely to move it into a designated space instead of across the backs of three cars parked properly, so I could get out. She decided after a little while of smirking and looking at the other teacher with a "Shall I?" look on her face. The other teacher, to her credit, looked embarrassed, but I could have crowned Faith. Just *who* did she think she was?

The next week was the last but one week of term before Christmas, so everyone was excited. Lots of the children forgot their manners and were rude and nasty to each other and to staff, so it wasn't a lot of fun. Lily, however, was settled and happy! One day in the week, the whole class went to Oxford for an exhibition about rainforests for the day on a coach. Lily went too, and her mum went with them, so I wasn't needed for Lily in the afternoon and had been asked to look after Andy instead to give his carer a break. However, he was unsettled and moody, so she decided she would stay with him herself as usual, and I was asked to help in class 4/5 instead. Lily's morning assistant was in school as usual, but with Lily away at the rainforest, she had a chance to read Lily's full history from her file, and she also made up some charts on the computer and laminated them for everyone's use—things like flow charts for earning her tokens.

I went into class 4/5 at 1.15 p.m. as arranged and was happily working with a girl who needed some support. On her table was a very disruptive boy who was giving me problems too, so I was busy and engrossed in what I was doing. I was annoyed at 1.45 p.m. to be disturbed by the morning assistant, as she wanted me to move my car for her so she could leave. I went with her, and she said she had had to move her car for Faith at 12.55 p.m. but that she had been so snooty and rude that she had wanted to report her to the head. I said that I often had similar problems with her and that I was going to mention it to the SENCO.

The next day was back to normal. Lily was on good form and settled in the afternoon, having loved her rainforest visit the day before. She had done all the work asked of her in the classroom in the morning for a nice change. At the end of the afternoon, she became a little upset and asked to go to the SEN room with me, so we went. There was a meeting going on in there, so instead we borrowed the whiteboard from the room and drew on it and wrote jokes on it in the foyer.

At home time, the children all filed through past us on their way out of school. Ellie came through too, and she came to have a look at what we were doing. She picked up the whiteboard rubber and began to wipe the pictures off the board, but I stopped her and told her that we were still using it and asked her to leave it well alone. We replaced the bits she had wiped off, and Lily and I went to get her coat, bag, and so forth ready for her to go home herself. Ellie sat on a chair sullenly and waited for her foster carer to come and collect her and her sister Rachel as usual.

Lily and I collected her things, and on the way back to the foyer, we heard her mum and brother coming up the corridor to collect her. Lily excitedly showed her mum the Christmas tree in the hall. Then she rushed through to show her our drawings and jokes on the whiteboard, but the board was pristine. Ellie sat smugly behind it as we stared at it in disbelief. Everything had been wiped off. I looked at Ellie, and she looked at me. Denise took Lily home, and Lily soon forgot about it, but I was furious. I asked Ellie if she had wiped the board clean, and she said she had. I asked her why, and she just shrugged and said, "I dunno." I was so annoyed that I told her off there and then, and she almost cried. I stormed off to get my coat. When I came back, she looked so wretched that I apologised and told her I was sorry for getting so cross with her, but that she *had* done wrong. I supposed she was just jealous because I used to have so much time for her but didn't now. She did seem very jealous of Lily—but then so did Annie, and she didn't spoil our things. Whatever her reason, I was annoyed with her.

The next day was again brilliant in the afternoon after a rough morning. I awarded Lily a sticker for her good work, and she excitedly told me that she had kept all her stickers from school and that this one was number eighteen! She said that they were all on her bedroom wall. At home time, I told her to put her shoes and socks on, since they were off when I got her in the afternoon (they often were), but she said her shoe was broken so she couldn't. I had a look and saw that she had ripped the straps off them. I told her to put her socks on anyway, and I got her some PE pumps to wear home instead.

Her mum was furious. She said that she couldn't afford any new shoes and that Lily would have to wear those PE pumps all holiday until she could get her some new shoes in January. I didn't get involved, but I was very surprised; I would have thought that because Lily was fostered, the fostering service would have bought her some new shoes if she needed them, for whatever reason she needed them.

On the Monday, Lily was resplendent in new shoes and was showing everyone them, so I didn't say anything about it. The SENCO had said that she was sure it was just Lily's mum being too proud to ask for financial help from the fostering service, so we just assumed she had asked after all. When I collected Lily from Liz at 1.15 p.m., I was informed that she was underneath the staging in the hall, which was for the Christmas concert, and that she wouldn't come out for anyone. I had brought a new magazine with me, *National Geographic Kids*, which I had taken to buying each month for her (with the head's blessing), as she always loved it. It seemed to be on topic curriculum-wise too, so it was very helpful and interesting. I showed it to Lily, and she came out immediately like a lamb and went into the classroom calmly, as if nothing had happened!

Lily went under the staging a few times a day after that, for most of the mornings of course and also in the afternoon if I wasn't quick enough to distract her. She discovered that one of the panels had hinges so she could pop her head up in the middle of the staging, and if the children were practising on the staging, then it got even more of a reaction, which she loved. It was terribly dangerous, but I couldn't stop her. In the end I started bringing in Charles's many *Beano* annuals for her to read, and she came out as soon as she saw those each day. It was bribery and corruption, but at least it worked!

She told me one day that she had seen her grandparents and was very excited about it. I asked her if they were just *her* grandparents or if they were her brother's as well, and she said just hers, so I thought she meant her real ones. Her mum, however, said that they were *her* parents, so not Lily's grandparents at all really, but they hadn't seen Lily since August, and it had been a wonderful weekend with the grandparents showering Lily (and her brother) with love and kisses, so it had been a brilliant visit.

Lily continued to go under the staging each day, but on the day of the Christmas lunch at school, she was very good and stayed in her seat for the whole meal, largely because I was sitting near her and told her to! Afterwards she went underneath again and had to be grabbed and physically carried out of the hall by two of the teachers because it was the day of the concert and she wasn't going to be allowed to spoil it. We spent the whole afternoon in the classroom on our own. Lily was originally going to watch the concert with her mum, but her brother was ill that day and not in school, so her mum didn't come after all. After the concert had finished, Lily and I read poems together in our cuddle chair in the foyer, and then we swept up pine needles from beneath the tree in the hall, which she just loved; it was great fun! When she got anxious after a while though, I wasn't fast enough, and she zipped out of the hall and disappeared. I found her in her "reward room", which was a changing room that wasn't used anymore; her other support assistant had allowed Lily to work in there sometimes in the mornings. I didn't use it, as I didn't feel comfortable shut away on our own like that, but they both liked it.

I knew she was in there, but I didn't want to go in on my own to get her out again, and so I asked a passing child to go and get me an adult so I could go in and get her. We went in together, and the other adult said I must be mistaken, as she *wasn't* there. It was very puzzling, as I knew she hadn't come out again! After a while, a little noise gave her away and I realised she was actually *in* the bottom drawer of the filing cabinet! I asked her to come out, not wanting to pull the drawer and maybe hurt her by mistake, and she opened it a crack and laughed at me and closed it again. We were amazed that she could fit in there at all! She went in there a few times after that, but then we turned the filing cabinet to face the wall so she couldn't, which made her very cross.

In the final week of term, we watched lots of DVDs in class, which Lily loved, so she was really quite settled. One day we were reading in our cuddle chair in the foyer instead when her mum arrived at 2.30 p.m. She was surprised to see us there, asked why we weren't in class and wanted to know what the class was doing without her. I told her that the class were doing PE in the hall, and she was cross, as she said that Lily had always loved PE in Dudley. She reached across, snatched the book out of my hands and demanded that Lily sit on *her* lap. She read a bit more of the story (I was all the while wondering why she was in school so early at all) and then exclaimed that *I* had made her late for a meeting with the SENCO. She chucked Lily off her lap and flounced off to the SEN room for her meeting. Lily dusted herself down and climbed back onto my lap for the rest of the story. It was a very strange happening!

Another day, in that last week before Christmas, I arrived to find that the morning assistant was off sick. Lily, I was told, had managed beautifully without her; she had gone outside to play at break time (which never happened when she was there, apparently), and she had also gone outside to play after her lunch (again, this didn't normally happen). I collected her from the playground for a change instead of from the computer suite, where she was usually spent all her lunch break, and she came in happily and settled for the afternoon in the classroom with no fuss.

I noticed a strange smoky smell around the hall, and I learned that there had actually been a fire in the morning, which had started in the boys' toilets; a hand dryer had overheated and burst into flames. Apparently the whole school had been evacuated, and Lily had managed brilliantly, along with Andy, Annie, Ellie, and all the others that one would expect not to manage that kind of thing at all.

I was just astounded that Lily had coped all morning with no other support assistant and with all that happening too! The SENCO and I concluded that Lily was actually better behaved in the mornings when her other support assistant wasn't there!

The smoky hall meant that the planned Christmas disco was cancelled, but no one seemed to mind. All the classes had parties in their own classrooms instead. Lily loved the party food and games; she enjoyed the dancing and even enjoyed going around the long way (missing out the hall) through the cold playground to get to the infants' section, where Father Christmas was waiting with gifts for all.

Right up to the last five minutes of the day, she was wonderful. Then she suddenly realised that it was almost home time and the party was over, and she started crying, saying that no one had told her it was the last day of term! She exploded with rage and threw everything she had at me, literally! Her mum eventually turned up, collected her from underneath the table in the science resources room, and dragged her away, kicking and screaming. I hoped they had a wonderful Christmas and a relaxing holiday, but I would have to wait and see!

CHAPTER 24

SPRING TERM

After Christmas, our time at school was rather difficult. Lily had no recollection of Christmas and denied having received any gifts. Her other support assistant was a little put out when the pink fluffy pencil case she had given Lily was eventually remembered but not attributed to her; Lily said mummy had given it to her, and we all wondered whether mum had taken our small gifts and said that they were all from her instead; we'll never know though.

Lily continually ran all over school and destroyed whatever she wanted to. Lily's mum came in for meeting after meeting, bringing various people to support her whilst she told us how wonderful Lily's behaviour was at home and how she was amazed at the trouble we were having with her. We didn't believe a word. It was as though she was worried that she would lose Lily if she told anyone that she was just as demanding and destructive at home. This was most unlikely! There probably isn't anyone else who would take her, truth be told, more's the pity.

There was one morning in particular which reinforced our view when Lily wrecked a window blind and was terrified that if we told Mum she would be cross again. It turned out that Lily had destroyed the living room curtains that day too.

We were promised a new quiet room where Lily could go when she was feeling stressed, which was just what we needed. The stationery cupboard was duly emptied and reinstated in the art supplies room, and we devised a new token and reward system to use alongside this new room, but we were thwarted when the builders took over six weeks to get it done for us. Just before the Easter break, they started decorating it at last.

After Easter, we started well. The room was ready, and Lily was very excited about it. However, it was painted blue, and the radiator had been completely covered with panelling (to stop Lily climbing), and there was no access to it, so the room was freezing, even though the weather outside was glorious. Lily started using the room straight away but soon got bored and wanted more things to do, which was when the new rewards system rolled into place. Lily had to spend fifteen minutes in class to earn a token. The reward was doubled if she joined in with the work with the other children. In the afternoons, the maximum she could earn was sixteen tokens, so I told her that if she managed over half (nine), she would get a reward time in the quiet room. She was happy to go along with this and was soon in class on the occasional afternoon and even enjoying the lessons and was delighted at having a session reading the *Beano* as a reward afterwards. Her other support assistant and I said that in addition, if Lily had a super morning or afternoon, she would get a slip to take home, for which Mum had agreed to give Lily 5p. She was happy to be involved and to be able to give Lily treats for schoolwork, as it reinforced everything at home too.

Lily didn't get many slips to start with, but one Monday she had earned one in the morning, which she was delighted about. Her mum was delighted too and awarded her 20p! The next day she didn't get one in the morning, but she did get one in the afternoon. Her mum clapped her hands with delight and promised Lily another 20p, along with a new dress, if she got three slips.

We were so annoyed that Lily's mum had deviated from the arrangement. We now had to be more careful about handing Lily the slips, as her rewards were way more than we had agreed. The next day was awful, and Lily was very angry when at the end of the day she realised that she hadn't got her third slip; she insisted that we didn't tell her mum what she had been up to and demanded a slip anyway, which was never going to happen. Her mum was very disappointed too, as they had been going to buy the dress straight after school. Lily was further frustrated because her little brother, having completed all that had been asked of him, did get his treat, and they went to buy him a new watch after school, and Lily just had to watch his pleasure.

On the Thursday, Lily did get another slip in the afternoon, as she had been so good, and although she had had a rough morning, I felt that it would have been unfair if hadn't given her a slip that day, and so her mum took her straight out to buy the dress after school. On Friday she got two slips, as it was an excellent day, but instead of the 10p we had agreed on, Mum whisked Lily off to an expensive local attraction straight after school. It made me wonder whether Lily's mum had received some funding, as she was suddenly so happy to spend lots of money on Lily, when usually money was very tight.

By Monday, Lily was so "treated out" that she just didn't care whether she got slips or not, and so her behaviour deteriorated considerably. She didn't earn any slips that day, but she did get one from me on the Tuesday, as she had an excellent afternoon in class.

On Wednesday, her other support assistant had arranged that she wasn't coming in, as she had a family funeral to attend, so I was asked to take over with Lily at 12.15 p.m. for her lunch hour and then stay on as usual, and another assistant was asked to take Lily for the morning, as she had managed well with her before and also looked after Lily during the Easter holidays. When I arrived, it was clear that Lily's morning had not gone to plan at all, as Lily was racing around screaming and laughing maniacally, and she was barefoot. She came to me when she saw me, and she hugged me hard and then ran off towards the computer suite, where I found her trying to put on a pair of gym pumps. The other assistant soon arrived and said that they were not Lily's but that she had taken them from year six's cloakroom. She also showed me a keyboard which Lily had broken during the morning.

I went and got Lily's lunchbox and swapped it for the pumps, which I replaced in the cloakroom when she was settled with her lunch. Quite quickly, Lily's class came to join her with their lunches, and immediately one of the boys decided to pick a fight with Lily; I was so annoyed with him! Then another one of the boys told Lily that he had made her a paper plane and told her to go and get it from the classroom. I didn't let her go, of course, and I asked the boys to stop disturbing Lily's lunch. When she had finished, Lily went to put on her shoes and socks at my insistence, and then she went outside to play.

Her play session went very well, so I awarded her two tokens for being in the right place and doing the right thing. After lunch, I got her back into the quiet room quite easily, and Lynne came to tell me that, after the morning they had had with Lily, I wasn't to let her out of the quiet room for any reason and that I was to press the new panic button if I needed any help.

Lily was calm and happy. We looked a book intended for very young children; we had looked at it many times, but Lily still liked it. I suggested rewriting the book as a poem—an idea that Lily loved, as she is very good at writing poems—and it went very well. When we had finished working out all the rhyming verses, I wrote it out neatly for Lily to illustrate. However, as I was writing, I was aware that Lily's attention had wandered, and she took the cushions off her chair next to me. I expected her to start throwing them at me. She did put them on my head so that they fell off onto the poem I was writing out for her, and then she dragged her chair back towards the door.

I got in the way, as I knew she was going to put her chair next to the door so that she could stand on it and reach the two handles at the top and bottom of the door; she had discovered that she could stand on the bottom one and push up the top one and open the child-proof door herself. She began to scratch and kick me, screaming, "Get out of my way!" so I pressed the panic alarm, as the head had told me to. An ear-splitting noise filled the room, and Lily looked horrified! The head came running and entered the room. I reset the alarm, and together we tried to calm Lily, but she threw whatever she could get her hands on at us. She ripped every sheet of paper she could reach into confetti and threw it everywhere, and she started spitting most unpleasantly. The head said she had to clear it all up before home time. Lily got even crosser, so we left the room and the head stood outside, holding the handles so she couldn't let herself out. I went to wash the spit off my face and clothes. Eventually Lily calmed enough for me to re-enter the room, and I saw that she had tipped the table over onto its side. She was lying behind it, pretending to be asleep. When she saw me, she started rolling bits of paper up into "ammo", which she piled up like snowballs ready for a snowball fight. I ignored her.

After a while, she started bobbing her head up and down, and each time she came up, she had a different expression on her face. I laughed and said that Charles did that too. She came over to me and threw her arms around me and hugged me, and I knew she was feeling much better, so I told her to tidy up the mess so that we could have some fun. She pushed all the bits of paper into a pile in one corner, and I sat by the pile and pulled out bits that were big enough to make paper planes with. Soon planes were whizzing all over the room and we were having a brilliant time. After that, Lily got two of the chair cushions and put them on my lap so she could sit on me, and we had a long, calm cuddle, which was lovely. Her mum came to collect her and was disappointed again that Lily had not had a particularly good day and hadn't got any slips, as her next treat was to be her mum coming in to have an art session with her for her next reward time, and they were both looking forward to that.

The next week brought a better opportunity for Lily to have a treat with her mum; her class were invited to go to see class 4/5 in a music competition at Warwick Arts centre on the Friday, and Lily's mum said she would go with the class so I didn't have to. I went in as usual on that day, but half an hour earlier than normal, and Lily's morning assistant and I were able to spend half an hour together talking for a change, and then I went home at 1.15 p.m. I knew I would have to make up the two hours, but I was already booked to go in on the next Tuesday at 10.30 a.m. to cover for the other assistant, as she had to take her mum somewhere.

On the Tuesday, I went in at 10.30 a.m. as arranged and took over with Lily at break time. She managed a good session after break and completed three pages of numeracy work (old SATs papers) before lunchtime. I was relieved by her class teacher so that I could have my lunch in peace, and after lunch I continued as usual with Lily for the rest of the afternoon. She went to the ICT suite and managed that lesson well, and afterwards she came back to the classroom as well. At 2.30 p.m. she suddenly needed to go to the toilet, and I inwardly groaned, as this was an oft-used diversionary trick of Lily's. However, she really did need to go, and by the time she arrived she had had an accident and told me her knickers had poo on them, so I phoned the school office with my mobile phone and asked the secretary to ask the SENCO to come and assist. She did and brought Lily some new knickers and a bag to put her dirty ones in. I asked the secretary to phone Lily's mum to take her home. Mum arrived at home time, after keeping poor Lily waiting for half an hour, and then said that they were going to the shops on the way home to get that night's dinner and bread for the next day!

The rest of the term passed in a similar way, and I was very glad when at last the summer holidays arrived and we had seven long weeks of holiday to look forward to.

After a few days off (it felt like!), we were into the new term. Lily's new teacher was new to the school so came in all organised and I even got a timetable emailed through to me on the preceding Friday. I was ready for Lily, having typed up the timetable and token sheet, and the Monday went very well.

When I arrived, I was a little early, so I went to find her in the playground, and Lily threw her arms around me. I spoke to her morning assistant, who was disgruntled, as she said that she hadn't had any work provided for her to use in the quiet room with Lily (for literacy and numeracy) as she had before, and that she was therefore having to make it up as she went along. She said there was no point in asking for any work, as Lily's old class teacher had taken over as head of maths from someone who had left. She had told us last term that she wasn't happy about making up any extra work for Lily on top of her other planning work.

At the end of the lunch break, Lily skipped into school and was very happy to show me her new classroom and her new pencil case. In PE that first afternoon, I was pleased that Lily even took part, as she usually didn't; often when the class began to get changed for PE, Lily would bolt, but this time there wasn't time to change, and we just had circle time together in the hall, which she was happy with. When each child was asked to say the best thing about being back at school, Lily looked at me, leaned across and placed her finger on my nose, and said, "Being with Mrs Patrick again!"

She stayed with her class for most of the afternoon except for after PE, when she said she needed a drink from the new drinking fountain in the girls' loos. I told her I would get her a drinking bottle from the office and asked her to stay where she was, but of course she had vanished by the time I got back. I found her in the quiet room, hiding behind the door, but she came straight back to the classroom to get her bottle, and then we stayed there as the class were dressing up as Victorians.

She enjoyed the whole lesson and earned enough tokens for a reward session, so we went to the computer suite for that. Unfortunately she couldn't find the site she wanted to play on, so she did get frustrated, but we went back to the quiet room, and I read her the beautiful short version of the Water Babies book that we had been lent, as the class was going to be having that book read at the end of each day.

Her teacher said that Lily hadn't been in the class in the morning, and she was so pleased that she was in the afternoon but added that she didn't know what she would have done if I hadn't been there.

Lily was reported to have bounced back into school on the Tuesday morning of the second week of the new term, apparently delighted to be back. Her mum came in wheezing a few minutes later, obviously having been running to try to catch up with her! We had had a teacher training day on the Monday, which was all about getting children into writing, and it was very interesting, but I was delighted to be back with Lily on Tuesday afternoon as well. Andy was back too, but he had stopped talking again, as was usual after a long holiday. He was totally mute all day and looked very unhappy when anybody spoke to him, and it was obvious that he had had six weeks of uninterrupted television.

Our afternoons together were wonderful; Lily was happy to be in class on Tuesday and Wednesday afternoons, and she got on with the work happily so we could then have a reward session in her new reward area. The changing room that had caused me such headaches during the previous term was now locked and unavailable, and her morning assistant had spent Monday making her a new reward area in the library, which was so much better for all of us.

On Thursday, Lily was out of sorts and had a horrendous morning, sending a bowlful of water across the PE hall floor and having to be restrained. She was obviously up for a fight with me when I took over, as she thought I was going to try to make her go into the classroom, so I didn't. Instead I said I was quite happy to spend the afternoon with her in the library, and once there, I kept her busy and spoke to her (she wasn't responding) about how pleased I was with her. I said firmly that we were having an "afternoon off" but that tomorrow (Friday) I was expecting her to be in the classroom as before, and I added that if she was, then we would go and get her a Head Teacher's Award sticker for having such a good first few afternoons back at school. She was happy and compliant, and to my relief, she was in class as instructed on Friday! We had a lovely afternoon that day; she had an art lesson and spent the time making her practice piece—a pop-out card depicting a tiger in a rainforest. I had put a flick book in my bag as well, as we had been discussing those during the previous term and I had found one at home; it was of a kingfisher diving into the water and catching a fish. When I gave it to her to distract her from a slight blip, she excitedly showed it to everyone and was delighted with it.

On the Monday, Lily's behaviour was atrocious. She had refused to do any work at all in the morning, had been loud and aggressive, and was upset all afternoon too, refusing to even make eye contact even with me for a change. We ended up just staying in the library again, her reading *Beano* annuals from my bag and me drawing her reading them. I didn't attempt to try to get her into class; some days it just wasn't worth the effort. I could see she was going to explode if I pushed, so I didn't. She realized I was drawing her after a while and was very pleased, and I unexpectedly got the Lily I loved back again, happy and chatty, loving being drawn!

Near the end of the afternoon, I suggested that we read a book together on our snuggle chair, just to see if she would, and she did, so she sat on my lap in our chair in the foyer, and I read to her. Her mum came through to collect her at home time, but she was none too pleased to see us happily reading together and forcibly extricated Lily from me. I went home feeling rather defeated and actually not very well with a tummy ache, and I ended up being rather ill at home and was then, unfortunately, off sick for the next two days.

When I came back to work on Thursday, Lily was in a high old state. The teachers told me that she had been like a whirling dervish for the past two days, behaving badly, particularly in the afternoons, and having to be restrained at lot. On the Tuesday when I had phoned in, the head had said she was going to send Lily home, but then apparently Lily's mum had said she would come into school instead. On Wednesday, a supply teaching assistant had been found, but she had a dreadful afternoon with a completely uncooperative Lily.

On Thursday morning, Lily had done nothing but drive everyone mad. As I arrived I was met with a relieved "Oh thank goodness you are here" from the secretary, but also with a "Please could you wait over here and not let Lily see you; there has been an incident" from the deputy head. I learned that Lily had been playing dominoes with the SENCO and her assistant and had ended up throwing a cardboard domino at her poor assistant and catching her on the eyebrow, where she now sported a stick-on stitch. Everyone was upset and scared; there had been a lot of blood, and Lily had reacted like a caged animal trying to escape. I was then asked to take over with Lily rather than look after Andy that day, so I did.

I found her in the head's office, squatting on her feet on the chair, showing her knickers and not caring, shouting that she was *not* going to apologise *ever* and that she didn't like that assistant anyway. She was very rude and unpleasant, and I wasn't very pleased with her. However, when we left the office, she was happy to go and get her lunch, and she sat and ate it happily enough, chatting to me in the dining hall.

She went outside to play after her lunch, had a lovely time with the older children, and came in on time too. We had a pleasant afternoon in the classroom as she had an art lesson, one of her favourites, and we did some more work on her pop-up tiger card.

Friday passed without incident, and on Monday I didn't really know what to expect. I was hoping that maybe we could cook, but first Lily had to have her piano lesson; it was later than last term, as another girl needed the first slot because she was gong swimming in the afternoons, just as Lily had the previous term. When we arrived for Lily's slot, having extricated her from the computer room, the piano teacher, annoyingly, had forgotten that Lily's lesson had changed times and had just started with another pupil, so Lily had to wait for another twenty minutes. We went back to the computer room, and she had her piano lesson eventually. Afterwards there wasn't enough time left to cook. Lily refused to go back to the classroom, so we wasted another afternoon in the library instead.

On Tuesday afternoon, I was expecting to see the SENCO, but she had arranged a meeting in school for the next day so had swapped days. We did manage to make flapjacks again, and Lily was lovely. Every now and again she would freeze, and when I almost expected her to run away, she instead threw her floury arms around me and just gazed up at me lovingly, delighted that we were there, together, and cooking, which she just loved. She distributed flapjacks to all the staff she liked (although she refused to put one in her morning assistant's pigeonhole), and we made up twenty-three little bags again so all of the children in her class could have one each too, as before.

On Wednesday, the SENCO came into school. When I arrived, she called me over, looking very pale and wan, and said that they had had a dreadful morning with Lily, who had punched her assistant and managed to slam a door into the SENCO's head as well, which had hurt. I was dreading the afternoon, but as before, Lily was sweet and lovely with me.

Thursday was another matter; the class had PE, and Lily refused to do that, and then they had ICT, and Lily also refused to do that. I didn't have very much left in my bag to keep her busy, and so I had a trying afternoon, with Lily deciding what she wanted to do and me just following her around.

On Friday, Lily was running around in bare feet when I arrived, with a very dirty face where she had drawn all over herself with a whiteboard marker—tiger stripes. I had taken in a *Beano* making kit—a box of leftovers from a present Charles had received a few Christmases ago that I thought might interest her. First, though, I was determined that she would be in class, so I was relieved when she did go into class first. The art teacher was running an art lesson, and to her credit, Lily did manage to produce a lovely card—yet another version of the pop-up tiger card, as that was what the class were asked to do. The problem with being in class was that it was such a mixed-ability group, and we had to go at the pace of the slowest. I found it too slow too, so it wasn't surprising that Lily didn't usually want to be there.

Lily loved the *Beano* making kit, luckily, and we made up a few cartoon strips together. At home time, Lily was still in her bare feet and still covered with black pen, so she looked a sight.

The next week was just awful. The SENCO was booked off sick for two weeks, as she was having an operation. Lily's behaviour deteriorated very quickly, and she refused to go anywhere near the classroom at all. On both of the Mondays, Lily absolutely refused to take any part in her piano lessons. I told her the lessons would stop if she didn't use them, but as soon as we went somewhere else, it was the same story: "I'm just not doing it *today!*" She wanted to have her lessons when she felt like it, and not when she didn't, and she refused to listen to reason.

Not having the SENCO to talk to was amazingly unsettling for both of us assistants, and the other assistant was having awful trouble in the mornings; Lily was destroying display after display whenever she was asked (or made) to go to class. Compounding the problem was that I was feeling very low in my own spirits—so much so that I went to see my consultant, who said that I was now in a bipolar depressive state, which was obvious to him but hard for me to recognise I *was* feeling very flat and tearful, but I'd been thinking it was just work. He reassured me that he could tell, and he was certain it was a bipolar swing—which was quite reassuring, even if it didn't solve anything!

People at work began to notice, and although I was terrified I would end up losing my job, after just a couple of days they were all falling over backwards to support me and help me; it was as if they had had a meeting and been told that I needed help—and perhaps they had. Lily didn't understand and played me up, of course. One of the other teaching assistants sent me a lovely Jacqui Lawson electronic greetings card to say she had noticed how unhappy I was looking and that she wanted to cheer me up! I would be hard pressed to find a more supportive team of colleagues, and I was very grateful.

I was very relieved that half term was coming up and I had to get through only a few more weeks. During the next two weeks, Lily continued to be awful, destroying more displays in school and even scratching the piano in the hall with a sharp stone one morning with the word "Electra" in huge letters all across the front. The head was out that day, but we all knew she would be furious when she saw it. Lily's mum was appalled and so annoyed with Lily, but actually it did our hearts good to see that she *could* get cross with Lily, since usually her reaction to these things was an airy "Oh well, that's Lily for you." She immediately confirmed that Lily would have no more piano lessons, to a "But ..." and a pout from Lily. The next day, Lily brought in a tin of wax polish and was made to polish the piano, but it didn't help much.

We all enjoyed our week off for half term, but it went much too fast, of course, and we were all soon right back where we started. I had been up to Kendal with Charles during half term, and while there we had scoured the charity shops for items Lily might like. I found a *Beano* annual that she hadn't read, and some bits and pieces for making friendship bracelets. Over half term, the caretaker had managed to rescue the piano, which looked much nicer when we got back to school.

On the Monday after half term, Lily was outside in the playground when I got to work. Andy wasn't in school, having missed the last week before the holiday too, so I was able to help the morning assistant a little. When Lily refused to come into school after the break, one of the lunchtime supervisors offered her a piggyback into school, and she delightedly accepted. He carried her right into class, and before she knew it, she was in the lesson.

She remained in class for most of the afternoon. I had dangled the carrot of the new *Beano* annual, and she was determined to get at it. She managed to make a poster for the sort of person she would like to be her leader, discussing the qualities of such a person quite happily with me. Afterwards we went and played with a stuffed cat in the hall. She wanted the *Beano*, but I said that I would bring it in on Friday, provided she did some work each afternoon. It worked like magic! Each afternoon, I had to remind Lily only a couple of times, and she would shoot back to the class and take part in whatever they were doing.

On Tuesday, she took part in PE for the first time in ages. On Wednesday, she completed a French activity sheet. On Thursday, she did PE again. And on Friday, she took part in art and covered a shoebox to make a refugee's lunchbox. I helped her, of course, but she did it mostly herself and made a good job of it. When ours was done, she proudly showed it to everyone in the class, and then lots of children asked her to help them, and she did. We went and had a look at the *Beano* afterwards but having managed to spin out the art for as long as possible, she had only ten minutes, so she didn't finish reading it. I made her a bookmark, put it in the Beano, and closed it up, expecting an outburst, but she was quite happy, having had a bit of a *Beano* fix, and she went happily home.

On Monday, I still had the rest of the *Beano* to tempt her with, so she went into class and took part in French (a colouring session, using a French colour words sheet) and stayed for RE, where we watched a video about Christianity and also heard a story read by the teacher. Lily was happy to stay and take part, and she finished the *Beano* just before home time. I then read it aloud to her, and it was obvious that she had skipped most of the words and just looked at the pictures.

Nigel had gone to Brussels for the week on a course for work, so I was feeling a bit shaky, but we had a reasonable week, although Lily didn't do much work since there wasn't a new *Beano*. She did do a little bit each day and got to read an old *Beano* as a treat most afternoons. I managed to tempt her to play another computer game one afternoon which was about making machines, and she enjoyed that, and it was at least educational!

The next week, I had been asked to work on the Monday for the whole day, which I did, but it was a shame, since Nigel, having arrived home from Brussels on the Saturday, didn't have to leave until lunchtime that day. Lily's morning assistant was on a Team-Teach course like the one the SENCO and I did the previous year. She had to go a long way for hers, apparently, while we had been lucky enough to go on a course at a junior school in Warwick.

Lily was so surprised to see me when she arrived, but we had a super morning. She was happy in class until about 10.00 a.m., when we went to the SEN room, and together we completed her literacy sheet, which was about whether the children thought having homework was a good idea or not. Lily stated that she *never* did any homework (which is true) but agreed that when she used to, she liked it because it meant that she had some time alone with Mummy to do it.

She had a piece of bread for break, which had been free, as I didn't know where she kept her tuck money. She didn't eat it anyway but just licked the margarine off it. Her buddies didn't show up as I was told they would, as they both forgot, which wasn't very helpful, but Lily was OK and quite chatty with me. We sat in the hall as she usually did. Then her teacher came and took over while I had a cup of coffee in the staff room. Lily then came back to the SEN room, and I went to get her numeracy task from year five. I was amazed when she was still there when I got back, and we did it together; it was a page of following directions. She had a treasure-type map and was told where she was starting and then given directions, such as "Walk 1 square to the west and then three squares to the south", and then she had to say where she had landed on the map. I did the writing for her, but she did it with ease.

Lily's mum came to take her for her lunch break, and I had my packed lunch in the staffroom. In the afternoon, the class were making 3D models of food for their WWII assembly—items that were rationed, such as bacon and fruit. Lily came into class OK and seemed quite interested.

Unfortunately her teacher was away for the afternoon, so we had our usual supply teacher instead, and she took so long explaining what we were going to do instead of just starting that Lily got very bored very quickly, and she left the room before the children got started, which was a shame.

Lily said she felt unwell anyway and was ghostly white, and she sat on her beanbag while I read to her all afternoon—something she didn't usually want me to do—and it was fine. Her mum said she'd eaten no breakfast or lunch that day, as she was anxious, so it wasn't surprising she'd run out of her usual energy.

She then had a most unusual day off, as she was very under the weather that day and had an upset stomach, but then she was back. Once again, Lily's behaviour deteriorated, and we were off again on a whirlwind of spitting, biting, and nasty behaviour, which got Lily nowhere except on her own in the quiet room. She damaged the cupboard doors, actually taking the door to the room off its hinges one morning somehow in a fit of rage, and I got an afternoon off, as she had to be sent home because we couldn't keep her safe.

She began to display worrying sexual behaviour, making her toys all mate with each other most graphically and insisting everyone have a look at them in their cupboard, where "sperm-taking" (her words) was happening. She gouged words into the paintwork on the cupboard doors with a pen: "Do not disturb, sperm-taking taking place".

Lily continued in the same way for another few weeks, and we were all despairing of getting anywhere fast with her. We now knew (as did Lily) that at the end of the term Lily was to be moving to a new foster home and family, as her behaviour was just too much for her mum and brother to cope with anymore.

Eventually, one day just before half term when I arrived at work, I was ushered into the SENCO's office to be told that Lily was being re-fostered *that day*. Her foster mum had had a complete mental breakdown in the head's office that morning and had to have arrangements made whereby she would be collected by her brother, and Lily was having to leave that day and not go back home with her foster family.

I was told to behave as normally as I could, not tell her, and keep her in the quiet room, as her foster mum was going to be going home very soon and nobody wanted Lily to see her in the state she was in.

Lily was as silly as usual but was delighted when she found that her mum had brought in her DS games console for golden time, as she hadn't been allowed to have it at school before.

I knew that a teaching assistant had been despatched to their house with a key and instructions to pack up all of Lily's belongings, and it was surreal playing with her new DS with her, showing her how to use it. She had a game called Animal Farm, and my son also had that one, so I was quite familiar with it. We called her character "Lollipop" and made her a base called "Home". I was unashamedly putting in the names I knew she would find a comfort when she recovered from her shock of being taken to a new home—if she hadn't destroyed the DS by then, of course.

Just before home time, she suddenly stopped playing and told me that she was leaving at the end of the term. She said she would never forget the friends she had made with us. I felt awful about not being able to tell her what would be happening in a few minutes, nor even being able to say goodbye, knowing that she thought she had another six weeks with us. I did manage to tell her how much we all loved her and hoped she would be happy in her new home. The foster team arrived just before home time, and Lily, racing up the steps from the toilets, recognised them immediately and just stopped.

She was quite shocked when she realised just what was happening, and she kept asking to go home to get her things but was mollified to find that her favourite teddy was there in the car, waiting for her. After reassuring herself that her new foster home had lots of pets, she left haughtily and without a backward glance.

I was informed that, of course, my contract had to end when Lily left the school, and so I was told I was being given a few weeks' notice and would be paid until the end of February. I applied straight away for a similar position at another school and was delighted to be offered the position. Although strictly I couldn't start until the second week in March, the head released me to start immediately, and I started a week before the February half term holiday.

CHAPTER 25

ROBERT

I met my new charge a few days into my first week at my new school in February 2010. We were in year three/four, and the teachers in the class I joined were job-sharing, and so we had one every Monday, Tuesday, and Wednesday morning, and the other for the rest of the week.

I spoke with the head about my condition as early as I could and found that he knew all about it and was very happy that I would be fine with them.

Robert was a very immature 9-year-old with pale skin and blue eyes, whose most pressing problem was a crippling anxiety about coming into school, and on the days when he did manage that, his anxiety about going home was just as bad.

He was taking medication to try to calm him at home (Ritalin) when we met, but was taking only ⅔ of his daily dose, as he also had a heart murmur, which meant that the medication was too strong if taken at full strength. Having had a pill in the morning, he was sometimes able to come into school, where he was given another pill at lunchtime.

His behaviour in school was usually fine, but we were told that on arriving home he often exploded and was angry and destructive all evening, and not able to sleep. His mother was exhausted, having had to spend most nights awake trying to calm Robert for a very long time.

He was the middle child of three; his elder sister, Amy, and his younger sister, Clare, were very able girls, both of them reading and writing fluently. Both sisters were very uneasy around Robert; he would state that he hated them both to the point of having to use disinfectant spray on anything they had touched, since he then felt it was contaminated. The family were all upset and worried about Robert. His dad was on the scene but scarcely at home, having a job that required him to work away; he was often late home, if he came home at all.

Robert's grandfather did a lot of work with Robert; he was able to calm him when no one else could and often brought him to school and collected him when Mum was working (as a nurse, she worked shifts which changed), while the girls walked home by themselves.

Amy was particularly upset around Robert; she remembered him being a normal toddler until Clare was able to start school. Clare had learned to read and write quickly, and Robert had realised how much he couldn't do. Once Clare had overtaken him at everything, Robert became anxious and angry.

I didn't get many chances to be with Robert at first, since he so often wasn't in school or went home at lunchtime. When we did have afternoons in school together, he was pleasant, well behaved, and popular with the other boys, and he enjoyed most of the lessons. When we did literacy, he obviously struggled, so I used those lessons to start him on a reading scheme (Wellington Square) along with a friend, which they both enjoyed.

We worked steadily through the first book along with a friend called Oscar, who couldn't read either and was rather disruptive. Robert was very used to being allowed to just say answers for someone else to scribe, but I made him do it all himself, and despite trying every which way to get out of it, he was obviously pleased with what he was doing himself, and he was thrilled when I said that this work would help him to learn to read.

Robert was quite good at numeracy and took a workbook home to work through on his own, completing one page in it each week. He brought it in each Friday to be marked and spent some time every day with a numeracy teacher one-to-one. The numeracy teacher had a lot of a week off when I first started, since there had been a death in her family, so Robert's work wasn't marked that week by her. I marked it myself and sent it home again for the next page to be done over the next week, which annoyed Robert (he was overjoyed at the teacher's absence and the prospect of not having to do any numeracy at home), and he then had an awful weekend. That was unfortunate, but I wasn't about to let him have a week off numeracy when he was so seldom in school any way.

During that first half term at my new school, I started helping out with an after-school club in which another teacher was teaching children to knit. I helped with that on Wednesday afternoons and enjoyed getting to know some of the other children in the school. The knitting teacher was overjoyed that I was helping her, as I could knit and help the children— especially a year-six boy called Pete who wanted to try cabling.

One Monday, I had been asked to work in the morning as well, as Robert's usual morning supporter had to be out of school that day, so I would be in school all day with Robert. He tried not to come into school at all ("But why? … Mum, you'll leave if I go in …") His mum said he'd done a runner already once from the playground, and we managed to get him inside only because Clare had to go into the infants' through a different door and we all followed.

Once inside, I steered him towards the ICT suite, where I introduced him to an interactive website full of amazing games to play and learn at the same time. He loved it, and it kept him happy until he'd calmed down. We then joined his class as they returned from hymn practice, and Robert and I looked at one of his books in literacy, and he was happy and settled.

After morning break, Robert enjoyed the start of Charity Week—a week when each class took it in turns to put on lots of stalls and each child in the other classes brought 10p to buy five raffle tickets, which they would then "spend" on activities. It was year six's turn that day, and they had put on lots of fun stalls.

We then went on to numeracy, although Robert tried to convince me that he didn't have to go, as he hadn't done his weekly sheet. He got rather agitated and kept calling out, "Look in my book! Look in my book!" Robert's mum had written that they'd had a busy weekend and Robert had been too tired to do his homework, which of course didn't wash with his teacher, so we sat down and did it in class instead of doing what the others were doing. Robert completed a page and a half before he went off to his lunch and I went home for mine.

In the afternoon, when we restarted after lunch, Robert was different; he was sullen and moody and refused to do anything at all in class. His teacher was really annoyed, as he'd enjoyed Charity Week and playtime during the morning and had done lots of maths happily, and she wanted him to do some work for her too! Whatever we tried we were met with a sullen "You can't make me! Nobody can make me!" The SENCO happened to be in school that day, so the teacher went to ask her advice, only to be met with an "I'm too busy; just follow the procedure." The procedure for removing a child from a class was to send them to a paired class, but since our paired class contained Amy, Robert's older sister, that wasn't going to work.

Robert just sat and stared into space all afternoon. The teacher and I swapped roles occasionally so that a different person asked him to work each time, but it was to no avail. Another teaching assistant in our class eventually asked him what he'd like to do, and he said, "Go to play on a computer," so that's what they did. Robert gleefully took the piece of paper from his folder that I'd put there for his use in the mornings, which showed him the website for the interactive games I'd showed him, and off he went.

The next morning, Robert didn't come to school, and his mum sent a message to say that he was too upset because we'd made him do too much numeracy the day before. He didn't appear on Wednesday either, and the teacher mouthed at me above the other children's heads, "He's still too upset ..." and pulled a disgusted face; she was so cross with him.

On the Thursday, I wasn't feeling well, and although I went into school, I was sent home, as Robert wasn't there anyway. Over the day, I developed a very sore throat, aches and pains all over, and a high temperature, so I was off work on Friday too.

We had our Easter break of a week off then, which was just right for me to allow me to recover from a bout of flu, and when we returned, I started running an after-school club of my own called "Have-a-go Club", wherein I introduced a small group of children to some unusual crafts. We met on Wednesdays and we had a go at glass painting, plastic tube–tying, making macramé owls, and folding Japanese dolls.

Our weeks together went on with little change; Robert more often than not was not in school, and so I worked with Oscar, who made rapid progress. When Robert was there too, he was usually compliant and quiet, although he tended to make mischief with the naughtier boys if I didn't watch closely.

The children in each class had a system whereby they took a green (girl) or blue (boy) sash with them if they visited the toilets in the afternoons, so that anyone could see if someone had already gone. It was unfortunately necessary to ensure that only one boy or one girl had gone at any one time, because if a second child joined the first, they seemed to find it impossible to resist and always messed around in the toilets and corridor. Before this system was implemented, children quite often came back soaking wet from playing with the taps or very late from playing by the lunchbox stands and wasting time. If they were caught by the head teacher out of class, then of course he would be very cross and would also berate the teacher for allowing it to happen.

Robert very often wanted to go to the toilet in the afternoon, obviously just to waste some time and avoid doing any work, and more than once he had been caught messing about outside the classroom and the teacher had been embarrassed when the head burst in very crossly. One of our supply teachers was once spoken to by the head about this, and she then told everyone in the class that there was to be *no* going to the toilet in the afternoons unless it was an emergency. Robert was absent from school for two whole weeks after this incident, and he was so upset and anxious about it. When he returned, we had to put in place a new system just for Robert. He was given three "time out" cards, which he used for toilet visits whenever he needed to go (really just for a breather out of the classroom), and this worked well.

For a while, Robert was off his medication to see if it would help him to cope with time outside school, and he didn't come in much at all while he got used to it. However, it wasn't long at all before he went back on it. I hadn't noticed any change in him when he was at school, but his mum maintained that he was a holy terror at home, refusing to wear any clothes, and eating only at 9.30 p.m.

Many meetings followed, and many specialists came into school to observe Robert when he was there. One morning there was a lady observing who saw him having a terrible time when he came to school that morning; he had refused to enter the building and had been manhandled into school by the SENCO, his morning helper, and the class teacher. He had been incredibly aggressive and kicked them all whilst screaming himself hoarse. The head commented later that he was not to come into school by the front door ever again; he had not been pleased that every parent on the playground had had a grandstand view of Robert's performance.

The SENCO was annoyed that the observer hadn't offered any help or advice. The teacher was traumatised, having not seen Robert at that pitch before, and Robert, by the time I got in, was oblivious, just as though nothing had happened.

Just before half term in May, there was another meeting in which it was said that Robert had a good chance of being accepted at Ridgeway, a special school in the next town, near to our school. The SENCO was pretty sure he wouldn't get in, but in fact he did, and his mum told us in June that Robert was indeed leaving us and taking up his place in September.

I went to see the head to ask if there was any chance of being able to stay on next term with another child, but he said he had no one for me. He said that if anything came up, I would be first on his list and he wouldn't advertise, which was nice to hear. But of course, I was now job hunting again.

I looked through the jobs section of the Warwickshire County Council website for local schools wanting a teaching assistant, and I applied for the three jobs I thought I could do. I decided to fill in the applications very thoroughly, and I wrote about my bipolar disorder and my own experiences as a troubled child in the experiences section this time instead of hiding it on the equal opportunities bit, which was how I had filled in my form to my previous school originally. Although I had got the position, the head there was later very cross as she said she hadn't been told properly, and the first she knew of it was when I was off sick for a week.

I said to Nigel that if I got any further interviews, then I wouldn't worry about admitting it openly again, as it was obviously not going to be a barrier to me working.

One of the positions was a one-term contract for working afternoons with a child who had Down's syndrome in a village not far from home, another was a year of mornings with a child with pathological demand avoidance syndrome (PDA), and the third was much further away, working lunchtimes and afternoons with an autistic child for a year.

I was asked for an interview straight away at the local village school, and my interview went very well. I was amazed and sad when I wasn't offered the job. I phoned the next day to ask for feedback on my interview, and the lady there said that it had been a very strong field, with two candidates standing head and shoulders above the rest of the field, and that I was top pick of the rest of them. There were two positions (morning and afternoon), and both had been offered, but the lady in the afternoon was going to meet the boy on Monday, and if she wasn't happy, then I would get a phone call. I felt upset and disappointed, but at least I knew I hadn't scuppered my chances by being so honest.

Anyway, when I got to work the next day, the head called to me to make time to go and see him at the end of the day, which I did, and he offered me another term's work with them. He said it wasn't with any specific child but as an "intervention" teaching assistant with a newly qualified teacher (NQT) in the juniors, this time working in the mornings instead of the afternoons; he wanted to keep me on, and he said that if, in the meantime, another more permanent position did come up, then I could be doing that the next term, and I was delighted, although I had reservations about the hours; my medication was knocking me out, and I was having trouble getting up in the mornings.

I asked if I could have a think, and he said, "Well, how long will it take you to think about it?" I explained about my predicament; I was worried about the situation with my bipolar medication. At the time, I was taking it at bedtime and then waking with a hangover from the sedative effects and struggling to get going in the morning. However, was I going to get up and go to work at 9.00 a.m. every day? Everything in me was screaming *yes!* But I knew it could be a huge problem.

When I spoke to Nigel that evening, he assured me that over the long summer holidays I could manage to reschedule the medication; if I took it in the afternoons instead, then I would wake up more alert, and I said I would try that. I was filled with hope and began immediately, taking 50mg when I got home from work and 200mg at 8.30 p.m. The next day, I felt the results already; I was up and about earlier than usual, so after work I went to the head and accepted his offer.

I also spoke to the SENCO, and she told me that there were four children in my new class who would need my assistance and support; however, none of them had an "educational statement", so it would be tricky. She told me their names, and I was able to pick them out during assembly by asking the teacher sitting next to me.

I went home with a spring in my step. Now I could relax and enjoy the rest of the term and the holidays; I would still be working afterwards. I felt even better when I eventually was called for interview for *both* of the other jobs as well. Maybe being bipolar wasn't going to hold me back after all. Phew!

CHAPTER 26

CHRISTMAS TERM

The first term of the new school year began for staff on a Monday, for the children on Tuesday. I went in for my new hours and arrived at 8.45 a.m., in time for a quick catch-up and cup of coffee before the staff meeting at 9.00 a.m. The meeting was very interesting, and I was keen to get started. After the main meeting, there was a meeting for the teachers of the juniors, so I asked if I could gatecrash that meeting and go with my new teacher to "get up to speed" with the juniors and year three. Everyone laughed and said that the speed of the juniors was sometimes breakneck and sometimes dead slow, but that I was welcome. It was so useful, as the timetable was discussed, as well as timings for such things as assemblies and playtimes (and whether or not I was expected to supervise playtime); it turned out that I was expected to have my break at 10.15 a.m. during lessons so that I could be outside at 10.35 a.m. for playtime for the children.

My husband, Nigel, had been unwell over the previous weekend; indeed, I had had to go and pick him up from his flat in Portsmouth on the Friday, as he'd been too unwell to drive himself home. We thought he had flu, and he spent the weekend trying to shake it off. He hadn't gone back to work on the Monday as usual but instead stayed at home, feeling very rough indeed. I couldn't wait to go back early on the Tuesday to get started, so it was a pity that it turned out that my husband was very ill and actually ended up being admitted to hospital that evening; we really had thought he had flu, but it turned out to be pneumonia, and he was in hospital for seven days. I was able to bring him home the following Tuesday; I had missed a whole week of school! But the staff, of course, were wonderfully supportive, and I was emailed each day and told not to even think about work whilst Nigel was so ill.

I actually started at work the following week on the Wednesday, and it was a baptism of fire; the NQT in our class was unwell and not in school, so we had a supply teacher, but the TA who had been doing my work thankfully stayed on to show me what I needed to be doing each day. At least the children all had their names on cards at their positions at the tables so I could start to get to know their names. I soon found my spot, watching over a little girl called Nicola, whose behaviour was rather erratic, and four boys—Barry, Joey, Joshua, and Kit—all of whom were work avoiders. The morning passed quickly and uneventfully. We took the register (more chances to learn names!) and then got on with literacy; the children started on a booklet that had been photocopied by the supply TA the day before, and I helped where necessary. I had my break and went out for the children's playtime, where I stood in the construction corner and talked to the TA from my classroom, and then I went back to our class for numeracy. As we neared the end of the morning, the head came in to see me. He wanted to know if I could stay on for the afternoon too, as another TA was off unexpectedly, in my old class. I was happy to say yes, but first I needed to check how Nigel was at home. I went home for my lunch, and he was OK, so I phoned the office to say yes, that would be fine.

The afternoon in year four was like old times, with a familiar teacher but with all new children. It was really great; there were four other TAs in there, but they were all one-to-one with SEN children, so I got to do all the running around and photocopying, which I enjoyed. The lessons were RE (we learned all about Peter's conversion to Christianity), and then the deputy head came to take the class for ICT, which was good. We started ICT in the classroom, looking at a copy of *First News*, and then we were in the ICT suite, and no one had any problems labelling up a mock-up of a newspaper front page all about animals.

I went home via town, as I had a couple of jobs to do, and then I relaxed with Nigel, who'd made me a welcome cup of tea. He had had lots of visitors that afternoon, so I needn't have worried about him!

The next day, I was in school bright and early. The TA showed me how to change some of the children's reading books, which I did, and then the supply teacher asked me to take two children out for supervised reading aloud. She gave me two of the children the SENCO had named, so I was able to get to know them a little better. We found a quiet spot and settled down. The little boy, Kit, read first; he sounded out each word well and really tried, but then, when it was the girl's turn to read to me, he was cross and kept talking to me over her, and so she started saying she couldn't read because his talking was "stressing" her. I have to say that her wind problem was stressing me too! She had sat and silently passed wind at least four times whilst she tried to read, but she wasn't really trying very hard; with every word I asked her to read, she would say, "I have *no* idea!" crossing her arms theatrically, accompanied with a little puff of putrid gas; it was stifling but also rather funny. After our allotted ten minutes, we returned to class. The teacher was horrified but also desperately trying not to laugh out loud when I whispered about Nicola's "problem" that morning; she clamped her hand over her mouth and her shoulders heaved silently as her eyes watered and she mouthed "Sorry!" to me between gasps. I was laughing too. I was so pleased when she turned the handles by the windows and allowed lots of lovely, cool fresh air into the classroom; it was such a relief! Not such a relief was the discovery that whilst we had been out of the classroom, the supply teacher had decided to get rid of all the name labels on the desks; they had been there a week or so, and she thought they weren't needed anymore.

At break time, I was pleased to see the teacher from my class the year before back at work again; she worked Wednesday afternoons, Thursdays, and Fridays, so I'd not seen her since before the holidays. We stood and discussed our holidays and watched the children. One of the older boys, I had noticed, had a very short fuse and was always being told off for hurting others, I knew his name, as I had heard him being told off so often the previous year. As I was talking to the teacher, I saw another boy sidle up to him, look around quickly, and deliver a stinging slap to Callum's bottom. It was so hard and quick that I actually heard it from across the playground.

Callum spun around, saw who'd hit him, didn't retaliate to the offender (as he was much bigger), but streaked off around the playground, bright red in the face, cannoning into others and pushing people over. Of course, he was spotted and told off soundly again by a teacher as usual and sent inside; I was able to fill the teacher in on what had happened, and the other boy was also spoken to.

After break, we had numeracy, and I knew by then that I was supposed to be in year four's classroom for that session, so off I went. Quite a few of our year-three children were in that group, and the teacher asked me to sit with the lowest-ability group. There she was again, my little wind blower, and I inwardly groaned. However, she must have visited the loos over break, as she didn't repeat the earlier performance, much to my relief. The children had circle time, where they were showing that they knew their number bonds up to ten. The teacher was asking for a show of hands for each question, such as "Who knows the number friend for number eight when we are making number ten?" The children sat at their group table with some photocopied sheets for them to work from, writing in their exercise books.

The three children on my table had only two sheets to work from, so Nicola and Joey had to share theirs, since Leah was on her own on the other side of the table and they were sitting next to each other. Nicola grabbed the sheet and put it up right next to her eyes and refused to share it; the other two wrote the date and their "WALT" (we are learning to …) from the board into their books while I asked her to put it down and do the same, but she refused. Once they were ready to start, I told her she could share the sheet or not have it at all. She crossed her arms again, her lower lip pouted, and she told me I was stressing her. I really didn't care! Eventually she began to write the date and the WALT. I ended up finishing writing it for her, as she was taking so long, and I helped them all with the sums. Leah managed four, as did Joey; Nicola, only two. I went home that lunchtime knowing I'd had a good morning, and I enjoyed my afternoon walk with our dog.

The next day in class, I changed reading books and helped with literacy again. I then had my break and went to the playground for playtime. The

161

head wasn't out that day, but the deputy head was, and he positioned me by the adventure playground. It was fun watching the little monkeys on the monkey bars and walkways and tyre swings. Only one child hurt herself; she did so by letting go with one hand and pulling the muscles in the other because she was hanging on with only one hand. I took her to a first aider, and she was OK with a cold compress arm band.

As we filed back into school after break, Nicola broke out of our line and rushed over to the boy who'd been slapped in the playground the day before and kissed him! It turned out he was her big brother. That explained a lot, since his behaviour was so odd and often aggressive (even without provocation); this gave me some insight into her spoilt reactions at being asked to work.

That day in numeracy, I helped my little group once again, and they were again looking at number bonds to ten. This time their work sheet had sums like "2 + ? = 10"; they had to write the sum out, inserting the correct number for the question mark. My group found it very hard, but we substituted the term "question mark" with "mystery number" and we shook our fingers, which made them all laugh, and they got on OK. Nicola managed six correct sums! The other two, eight each. I was delighted with them.

I went to see the head of English at lunchtime because the deputy head had put a timetable for me in my pigeon hole, wherein he had asked me to take a small year-three group for extra phonics work each morning from 9.00 to 9.20 a.m., starting on Monday, and also some children for one-to-one intervention each day from 12.00 noon to 12.15 p.m., working on their reading comprehension. She was able to give me lots of books and worksheets and flashcards to use, as well as the whole timetable of phonics and comprehension subjects I was to use with them. I went home with a huge folder full to look through and use to prepare for the week ahead.

On the Monday, our own teacher was back (hurrah!) and feeling much better. The first thing she said after we'd changed pleasantries was "Where have all my name labels gone?" I told her the supply teacher had removed them but that she was welcome to put them back, as I needed them too, and she said she would.

Having diligently studied the folder and book I had been given, I was armed with all that I needed to get on with my phonics group on Monday, so I dutifully took my five children out of the classroom. We went into the ICT suite, as it was empty, but, annoyingly the caretaker had left a CD player running loudly, playing some rock music, and it took me a few minutes to figure out how to turn it down; I couldn't find the off switch, as it was on a shelf higher than I could reach without standing on a chair, and with a group of children watching, I wasn't about to do that! When I turned around, all of the children had hopefully settled themselves at a computer. I asked them all to come and sit on the carpet in front of me instead. Nicola was nursing a sore knee (she'd fallen over on the way to school), so I allowed her to sit on a chair. There was an immediate uproar: "Miss! Miss! Nicola's on a chair, Miss! I want to sit on a chair too, Miss!" On and on they went. I stopped them by starting to show my phonics cards and using them to communicate with the children; I had lots of sounds, including "ow" (*Perfect!* "What Nicola said when she fell over this morning"), "oi" ("What I will start saying to you, Kit, if you don't listen."), "ee" ("The end part of the word 'knee'), "j" ("This one's in your names, Joshua and Joey") "sh" (self-explanatory.), "oo" ("oo, I would like it if you'd just listen"), and "er" (*Yes* Well done, Connor, this one *does* say 'er'; all the others to which you just said "er" to weren't right, but this time you are"; this made us all laugh).

We went back to class a little late, but the teacher was also running late, so it didn't matter. I sorted out the reading books for the reading group for that day, changed their books, and wrote up the folder. Then it was time for my coffee break, so I went through to the staff room. Other TAs were soon arriving for their breaks too, and we all laughed when one said to another, "Oh, I love your new shoes!" and three people immediately said, "Oh, thank you!" There were four very red faces when she made it worse by looking along the line of proffered new shoes and chose the pair she liked most!

In the playground, the head directed me to supervise "down", which meant the assault course, monkey bars, etc., where I'd been on Friday. All was fine until one little girl, swinging herself happily by two hands, was "helpfully" given a push, as though she were on a normal swing, and she let go on the apex of her swing; she landed hard on her bottom and hands, which were behind her, having missed the wood chippings below the monkey bars, and she screamed. I took her to the first aider, and together we had to examine her bottom (which was already covered with a spreading livid bruise), check her wrists, etc. She was a little girl with lovely brown skin, but she had gone deathly pale from the shock and so was given a cold compress to sit on, and her mum was called. She actually stayed at school, as she was OK, but she was given a cushion to sit on in class and a pink accident slip to take home at the end of the day.

After break I went to my numeracy group and helped my group again. This was the same group as I had for phonics, so they were hard work! They all did quite well, and Nicola beat Joey by one question (she had ten right; he, nine) and he almost ripped his book up in his frustration, but I stopped him and talked about not talking so much and wasting time. They all did better than on Friday, so I was very pleased with them. So was the teacher; she said, "You have the hardest group; I hope your enthusiasm lasts!"

I took my first one-to-one reading intervention boy at noon, a boy called Ned in year five whom I'd never met before. He was delightful. He was reading a Horrid Henry book and was on the last few pages, so we finished it, and I was able to see that he understood it very well. When he'd finished, he proudly told me it was the first book he'd ever read from start to finish by himself. The teacher had asked me to concentrate on speech marks so he would be able to use them in his writing, which I did. He finished his book at 12.10 p.m., so I went back to my class and stayed to the end of the morning with them. I showed the teacher the spellings sheets that had been handed out the previous week in her absence, and we discussed them, and then I went to see the secretary. I wanted to know whether I was going to be paid for my week off. It turned out I was not, and therefore I needed to claim for the extra two hours I'd done on Wednesday of the week prior. That done, I went off home for my lunch, having had another successful day.

On the Friday of my second week back at work, my routine was settled: 9.00 to 9.20 was phonics with my little group of five: Nicola, Joey, Connor, Kit, and Joshua. Nicola was my little windy girl from the first week, and she was also in my maths group. Joey was a coloured boy with a big attitude. Connor was a quiet Caucasian lad who was really quick at phonics, quiet and unassuming, always first to tell me a sound from a flashcard or to write down a sound I said. Kit was a mouthy loud boy who didn't understand the suggestions that he should stop talking, playing, messing around under the table, or running around the room when I asked him to. Joshua was an Asian-looking boy with huge black eyes, a mop of black hair, and an attitude to beat all the others. He was also the son of one of the other TAs in school, so I was wary of telling him off too often in case he complained to his mum—a situation I wanted to avoid at all costs.

Unfortunately, Joshua understood everyone was afraid of upsetting his mum, and he got away with murder. In the first two weeks, there was no sign of a reading folder from him, so I couldn't change his reading book. He was dismissive when I asked him for it, saying confidently that he had lost it so wouldn't be bringing it in again. I arranged with the teacher that the next time it was his turn, I would send him a book home, the next one on his list in the reading folder I had, in a temporary folder with a note to mum to ask her to help him find his own folder or replace it with a new one, and to replace the missing reading book. I was going to do this with all of the children who hadn't brought their reading folders in yet, not just Joshua.

On the Friday in our phonics group, Joshua was as revolting as usual, sitting under the table with Kit, giggling at some joke and ignoring me. They enjoyed our sessions, as it meant they could be out of class; they thought it was a free session. I warned all of the children who were messing around, and I began a countdown. "Kit and Joshua, come out from there and sit on the carpet in front of me … Five. Joshua, stop talking, look at my flashcard, what does this say? … Four. Joshua, I want you to write down another word with 'ay' in it … Three. Joshua, stop talking … Two. Joshua stop talking … One. Right, Joshua, I want you to go back to your class; you are not listening, you are not joining in, and you are disturbing my lesson. Off you go."

There was a stunned silence, and then Joshua began blubbering, "Oh, I'm sorry, Mrs Patrick; I won't do it again. Mrs Patrick, please let me stay."

I said, "You are right Joshua, you *won't* do it again—not in this lesson. We'll try again on Monday. Off you go back to class." I stood at the door and watched him trail wretchedly back to our class. Another TA appeared and asked him what was wrong. I said that I had asked him to go back to class, and she gathered him up in her arms, looking at me with daggers in her eyes, and said, "Come here, Joshua; tell me what's wrong, darling …" I retreated into the ICT suite again and got on with my lesson, my face burning.

Very shortly, the other TA popped her head around the door and said, "Please may I talk with Kit and Joey, Mrs Patrick?" and she took them away.

They soon came back, visibly upset. Kit was saying over and over, "Mrs Patrick, I was the one who was talking to Joshua; he wasn't talking to me." I got on with my lesson and asked him to stop talking, over and over again. He asked "Is Joshua going to be in our group tomorrow?" I said that yes, Joshua would be with us again on Monday, and that they should all learn the lesson that I was talking no nonsense and that anyone who consistently disrupted my lesson would be sent back to class.

When we went back to class, Joshua was glowering at me, but we carried on as usual. They were having their literacy lesson, so I helped support them as usual. The teacher had split my group of needy children up and scattered them around the room, as they didn't really get on well and their table was always very difficult. She asked me to support Kit and Nicola's tables, as those two children were sitting back-to-back, one on each table.

The children were writing a poem using adjectives and similes. Kit's was about spiders. He had already written, "Spiders make webs and they eat bees and flies." He asked me to help him with some more adjectives, so we came up, together, with "They are black and fierce, and they have eight eyes", which I thought was lovely.

A little girl on Nicola's table was asked to read her poem out, which she did, and the children were all told to put down their pencils and listen. It was about butterflies and their colourful wings, mentioning that they are as pink as roses (her simile); it was very good. I noticed that Kit was obediently turned in his seat and watching her, and listening intently, so I was quite surprised to see his neighbour, Joel, quietly reach past him, pick up his red pencil and substitute his own camouflage-patterned pencil; he held Kit's pencil under the desk on his lap. When Kit turned to start writing again, he picked up his pencil, looked at it in a puzzled way, looked through his pencil case and began to look around his chair on the floor. I asked him what he was looking for, and he said, "My red pencil … I'm sure my pencil was red."

I said, "Joel's got it, haven't you Joel?" Joel went bright red and nodded in embarrassment. He passed it back to Kit, who gave him his own pencil back. I looked at Joel and simply said, "Joel, that wasn't good, was it?"

I went over to the teacher and whispered what had just transpired. She looked surprised and said, "Well, there's been a lot of that going on. I'll have a talk to the whole class before lunch. Thank you, Mrs Patrick".

I went for my break at ten fifteen so I could help with outside play, and the other TAs also came for their break. The TA who had spoken to the boys was clearly enjoying my discomfort; she waited for everyone to come to the staff room before asking me just what had happened in my phonics group. I explained how rude Joshua had been, that I had warned him over and over, and that I had then carried out my threat. She said that he had cried and denied everything, blaming the two other boys, saying that they were being mean to him, but once she had sent them back to my group in the ICT suite, he had changed his tune, run back to her and said, "It *was* me; I was rude and didn't listen to Mrs Patrick. I'm sorry!"

I was still waiting for his mum to appear and lay into me, but then someone said, "Oh, don't worry; she's off ill today." It had been her fortieth birthday the day before, and we had all had cake, and she'd had some helium balloons to celebrate and had obviously had a night of it. I couldn't have chosen a better day to sort Joshua out, and I was grateful.

When I went back to class with my group after break, we had numeracy, and Joshua asked me very politely to help him with his work, which I did, and he was lovely for the rest of the morning: "Yes, Mrs Patrick", "No, Mrs Patrick", "Three bags full, Mrs Patrick". It was delightful.

I popped back into our class at the end of the morning to get my bag to go home at lunchtime, and the teacher was sitting marking work. She said, "Do you know, we've all been thinking it was Nicola who's been taking things, because she was caught doing it lots of times in year two in the infants' class. She used to ask to go to the toilet and then go through everyone's bags, taking stuff she wanted. She was caught a few times. I had no idea it might be Joel"

I spent every morning that term with my group for phonics. They all progressed really well, and soon the teacher was commenting on their marked improvement with their reading, which was lovely to hear. We went through all the sounds on my sheets, getting progressively harder, and then, at the start of the next half term, we went back to the start to check that the basics hadn't been forgotten.

We had gained another member of our group, Cory, a boy who the teacher thought would benefit from extra phonics, but who, not having been with us from the start, was keen to assert himself and disrupt my lessons. We were all finding it harder by now; the novelty had worn off, and phonics was as much of a challenge as the rest of the morning with my difficult group, but we struggled on. I began to take Joey and Nicola out after maths for extra work; I had them do their maths homework and their comprehension homework for the teacher too, since neither was managing it at home, and they were both falling behind. At the end of the term, I was feeling quite demoralised with my group; they had reached a plateau, and I was struggling to interest them as I had been able to at the start of the term.

The head teacher had not been able to promise me any further work once my term's contract ran out at Christmas, I had started asking at half term, and it was a few weeks of uncertainty for me, but finally he decided that he would be able to keep me on for a further term, up until Easter 2011, although he couldn't promise what I would be doing. He later informed me that there was another position which had a vacancy in the afternoons the following term, which he encouraged me to apply for.

I had been filling in for ill colleagues and had often been asked at short notice to work all day, usually with a boy in year two, Joseph, an extremely high-functioning autistic boy with no social skills at all, so I had been staying for a cooked lunch with the children and then carrying on all afternoon, and I found that I quite liked that arrangement. I thought about applying for the position. If I was successful, it would mean that my usual morning's work would be supplemented by also working every afternoon, this time one-to-one work again with an autistic child. I tried to work out which child it was to be with, hoping it wasn't such a challenging child as Joseph!

As it happened, my low mood deepened, and I became quite unwell with depression again. It took a few weeks of antidepressants to bring me back out of it, by which time I had flunked the interview, but it didn't really matter; I was quite happy staying as I was with my class and phonics group. The child concerned did turn out to be Joseph anyway, and I really didn't want permanent afternoons with him at that stage. Then I was given a new child to help with his reading, another boy from year six, so my usual Monday and Tuesday boys doubled up on Mondays, and I had him on Tuesdays and the usual lad on Wednesdays.

After a while, things began to improve; Joshua was diagnosed as dyslexic, which was what we all suspected, but his attitude just got worse. He was sullen and rude—not a nice boy to have around at all. It meant, though, that I could help him more and not feel that he just wasn't trying, which was how it looked, I had to admit! My new year-six boy began to get interesting to talk to; he knew lots about nature and birds, so we often talked about those sorts of things, which was lovely. I was able to bring it back to reading by bringing in my own nature books from home so we could look at them together.

One day, when we least expected it, Nicola and her brother Callum stopped coming to school, and we learned that they had gone to a safe house to avoid Mum's boyfriend. It was a worrying few days, but we had to think that it was for the best. There had been gossip that they had been taken into care, but that wasn't it at all. After a week and a half, they came back. Nicola was just as filthy as usual, and the staff running the breakfast club started taking them off for breakfast before school, as it was obvious to everyone that they were both really hungry. Such a shame.

Life carried on as before, and I was now wondering about next term: would I be staying on for another term or not? The head couldn't tell me; he explained he was going to numerous meetings with governors, the budget was really tight, and I could see that he was getting fed up of me pestering; I only asked once a week, but I started at half term, and by the last week I still hadn't had an answer. Finally, he came to find me and said he couldn't offer me another term after all. I was so disappointed, but then he laughed and said I was staying on for a further *three* terms—a whole year!

We were heading nicely towards Easter now, and I was also running a craft after school club called Have-a-go Club. We made palm crosses and Easter cards; Nicola being especially pleased with hers. The very next day, she was not in school again, and I was told that they were again in a safe house to avoid Mum's boyfriend. The head was of the opinion that the family should stay away for good this time to avoid such disruption to the children, but it wasn't up to us.

Easter preparations went on; the children performed their term's topic as a concert titled Volcano!, which went down very well. The children made their Easter bonnets for their parade on Tuesday afternoon, and we all went to church in the morning at our own St Paul's church, just a short walk away.

CHAPTER 27

SUMMER TERM

I carried on as before, although I was sad to note that Nicola did not return this time. I had badgered and pleaded with the class, and by now most of the children were reading regularly again; I had to resort to sending home a temporary book to remind parents only once in a while. It was a method I had tried before with success, and the teacher was happy for me to use it here too.

I was asked to cover for a sick colleague who worked at lunchtimes, so I started doing an extra hour each day straight away. It was quite fun; I took a class worth of sandwich eaters to the Wild Area each day on a rotary system so everybody got the chance to go, and it was lovely sitting and talking to the sixteen or so children each day and watching the others on the playing field. When they had all finished their lunches and gone off to play, I went into the hall and started to sweep the floor, at least picking up the biggest bits. When the last child left the hall, I went out onto the junior playground and field to cover the corner, where a group of boys were making a den under a tree. It was all quite idyllic and reminded me of my own times playing in woods when I was young.

The school had magnificent facilities: a huge field with a den area; poles and material for making tents and such; the Wild Area, a small area with benches around in a circle and bushes planted all over it; a golf course made by the children for the children; an area on a bank where boys dug deep grooves and poured water into them from the drinking fountains to make streams; plus tennis nets, basketball pitches, and endless sporting equipment (ropes, balls, hoops, tennis racquets, quoits, etc.)

Lunchtimes were always fun, but we had our fair share of problems; even though we were super vigilant, sometimes someone was silly and we ended up with a broken wrist or strained ankle; it was all part and parcel of playing together and didn't happen very often. The head was sensible; he allowed the children to play freely. When the boys would make guns and start shooting each other, we didn't call their parents to warn them of suspension as you may have read about in the papers, because, as the head said, these boys all knew people who were actually at war right now, and many of them would go into the forces; it's only natural that they should play games of war, and so they did. Such an attitude is like a breath of fresh air these days!

After half term, I was back at work for just one day before I had a car accident and suffered a whiplash injury which was to keep me off work for three weeks; it was very painful and frustrating! A young lady behind me managed to drive straight into the back of my car when I was waiting in a queue at traffic lights. She didn't even try to brake, and subsequently the car behind her crashed into her rear too, so I got two hard jolts. I was very shaken up, but we exchanged details and I managed to drive home, as I hadn't got that far on my way to work. I phoned school to tell them I wouldn't be in and why, and then I was feeling so sore and stiff I thought I'd better take myself off to Accident and Emergency, which luckily is just a five-minute walk from our house. I was examined and found to have a whiplash injury, as I expected, but no broken bones or anything else, so I went home with anti-inflammatory drugs and painkillers. I couldn't turn my neck at all and was extremely stiff. I couldn't do anything around the house; I couldn't walk my dog or drive the car. I was stuck in the house for weeks. As it was entirely her fault, her insurance sorted everything out, including inspecting my car, which was a write-off, and arranging for compensation to be claimed for me.

We had been looking into buying a new car in any case, so a few weeks later I went to our local Nissan garage to look at their new small car, the

Pixo, which would be fine for me to get around in and for Charles to drive once he'd passed his test. They had a brand-new one in their garage which had been registered the previous year, and so they knocked off £1,000 and we bought it.

After three weeks, I was mobile enough to drive again and went back to work. I learned that I was to be teaching assistant for another newly qualified teacher after the summer holidays in one of the three mixed year-three-and-four classes, which I was excited about. I was really enjoying being a teaching assistant in a class rather than a one-to-one support teaching assistant, although I was also supporting individuals wherever necessary.

During the summer holidays, we went to Sweden to visit the World Scout Jamboree with Charles, as he hadn't got a place to go as a participant. It was great fun, Sweden was lovely, and the holidays passed quickly, as usual.

CHAPTER 28

ANOTHER CHRISTMAS TERM

My new class was full of children I didn't know; a lot of them were year threes so had been in infants the year prior and I hadn't met them before. A few were familiar to me from year three the previous year, who were now year fours. I had a different phonics group, with all new children to me, but I was teaching the same Phase 5 Phonics stage again. My new teacher was a very tall (6'2") young man, and he was lots of fun. I was still changing the class's reading books each day and supporting a less-able table, and we also had a one-to-one teaching assistant with us who was there to support Harpal, who I had had in my class the year before.

Almost at once, I was asked to also support a boy in year two, in the infants' section of the school, at lunchtimes. I collected him from the hall each day after his lunch and then supported him in the playground. Stuart was an angelic-looking child with light brown curls, blue eyes, and olive skin. He was always laughing and a lot of fun, but he had no social skills. He would march up to the boys playing football and just pick the ball up and then run into a corner hugging it, laughing, and saying, "It's *my* free kick!" over and over, infuriating the other children. It took me a few days to show him how to play properly, and he even began to score goals and was getting popular with the other children at last, most of whom—as usual at this school, I found—were very forgiving. After a week I was told that he wasn't allowed to play football because of the fuss he always made, but once the other members of staff saw that he was playing more or less properly, he was allowed to continue. I do wish people would tell me their rules before I am asked to take care of a child! Mind you, if they had, I wouldn't have been able to help him join in, so perhaps it's a good thing after all!

Half term arrived, and we started back on 31 October, with the children excited about trick or treating later, and the first day back was on the theme of chocolate. Each table had a packet of chocolate buttons on it, and once the children had eaten them, they had to compile a list of words to describe what it was like, using each of their five senses. Then the children wrote poems using their words, and they were very good indeed. After break they had more chocolate! In maths, the whole class sat in a circle, and each sampled a square of first plain, then milk, then white, and then chilli chocolate. Then they made tally charts of everyone's favourite, followed by a bar graph of their results. The children were quite high and silly, but it made for an interesting first morning back, and it went quickly. Stuart was pleased to see me too; his playtime passed without incident, and I was off home again, clutching my pay slip for October. I had been paid an extra £100 for my hours with Stuart, so I was very pleased.

On the Friday of that week, in the infants' playground, I had a horrible experience. While walking around the playground, I suddenly had a sense of something behind me and turned in time to see a little girl falling backwards off the front of the wooden ship and onto the bench seat inside it, landing on her back and head. I rushed over to her; she sat up and almost fainted and started screaming. I sent a child to get me the other lady in the playground, who came straight away, and we tried to get her to move to the first aid area, but the little girl wouldn't move. We sent a sensible child to get us the official first aider, but he came back and said she'd sent him away, saying she "was having her lunch." I went and found her myself; she was having a chat with someone in the hall. I said, "This is really an emergency; please come," and she ran to the playground. Once she'd laid Milly down flat, she called for a phone. I was the only one with one in my pocket, so I called the ambulance. I had also spotted the head once the first aider had got to Milly, and I informed him of what was happening. He was very concerned but was happy to let us deal with it. The ambulance got there very quickly, and Milly's aunty also arrived, and she was taken to the ambulance on a stretcher and off to hospital. I was in shock, so I had a cup of tea before I left for home that day. It was not a nice experience!

A couple of weeks later, I caught Milly standing on the bench in the ship with her arm hooked around the mast, spinning round and round. She didn't like it when I asked her to stop, and she said she wouldn't fall. She kept going. Her eyes were glazed, and she was wobbly, but she wouldn't stop, so I got in the way and physically stopped her. She said I was spoiling her game. However, when the bell went at the end of play, she suddenly launched herself at me from the bow of the ship. Luckily I caught her, and she hugged my legs and then grabbed my hand adoringly and said she wanted to stay with me all afternoon! I held her hand, and Stuart rushed over, full of jealousy, and took my other hand, so I took them both into class.

Later that term, we had a day when the teachers were on strike, so the children had a day off and it was just eight of us teaching assistants in school, and we busied ourselves. I did a huge pile of photocopying and laminating, and then we all made Christmas decorations; the staff were going to decorate the whole school after hours on the Thursday. (Unfortunately, I couldn't help, as I had Cubs that night.) On the Friday morning, it looked wonderful, like a winter wonderland with snowflakes hanging from every tile down the corridor and snow scenes and Christmas trees on every wall. Christmas music began to be played during literacy, and the infants practised their nativity in the hall. A lovely atmosphere pervaded everything, and all the children were happy and excited.

The rest of the year passed happily too; at half term during the spring term, the weather decided that it was spring after all, and the children put a spurt on in class to match, and everyone was doing really well. Stuart gave me a bear hug each day after lunchtime play by then, and I gave him stickers if he had had a good playtime (usually) and only had to move him down the behaviour board occasionally. I had asked the head if I was to continue after Easter, when my year's contract ran out, and he'd said his intention was to continue as before. I shortly received the news that I was to stay on for another year's contract, which was wonderful.

At this time, we decided that my mum needed to move to a new house from her little cottage to be nearer to me. Her cottage sold quite quickly, and I found her a wonderful ground-floor apartment in our town, and that made my life much easier; I could see her every day, as she was only five minutes' walk away now. She loved her new home, and as the year progressed she began to try crafts such as knitting (too difficult, as she couldn't see what she was doing), crochet (ditto) rug making with wool and a latch hook (which worked but was very difficult), and making a lovely rag rug, which was a great success. Over the first year, I knitted her a new jumper and one for myself, both to the same pattern except hers was green and mine a dusky pink. I knitted every evening at her apartment, and she enjoyed seeing the jumpers grow. I also knitted clowns from a pattern I'd bought for 20p at a fete and a hat and gloves from a pattern Charles had given me for Christmas.

We had a new boy in our year three/four class in April. Riley was from Germany and had an older sister in year six. He was delightful; I was asked to take him out of the class to see where his reading and writing skills were, and he was excellent at both. Whilst writing about himself, he used the word "because", and he used the familiar spelling strategy to help him. He started saying "Big elephants" but then got stuck. I prompted, "Can always …" He didn't like the word "understand" for the *U*, so we used "upset" and then "small elephants". He said he knew another word strategy for another word, so like a fool I asked him what it was and got (with him having a real twinkle in his eye) "Spiders have itchy toes."

Having a boy from Germany starting with us brought out the expected jibes about the war, but only from children who I wouldn't have thought considered themselves British: Harpal, in our class, from Indian stock, and Ibrahim, in year six, whose family were from Afghanistan. This needed careful handling, and at the next staff meeting, our teacher felt he had said enough to both boys to nip it in the bud. We would have to wait and see what happened from then on. We also had a new boy in school, Marley, a French boy who had no English at all. Luckily we had a number of teachers who could speak French well enough to be able to converse with him. I ended up supporting him on Fridays in maths and was pleased at how much French came back to me.

I had also started supporting a boy in year five, Trent, who was having emotional outbursts due to a complicated home life. I was asked to support him on two afternoons a week, of my own choice, to give his teacher a much-needed break. I went into his class each Tuesday and Thursday afternoon and supported him through science and history sessions; he was well behaved and loved having a TA all to himself.

The head then announced that he was to retire at Christmas, shortly followed by our deputy head, who had secured a headship at St Patrick's Primary School in Leamington, which, incidentally, used to be called Cashmore Primary School and was where I had attended as a child. Our deputy head was starting his new job in September, so it was going to all change in school very quickly. I just hoped that I had done enough to continue working at St Paul's under a new head; it was such a lovely place to work, and I wasn't sure I wanted to start again somewhere else. Our year six teacher stepped up as acting deputy head, so things would remain familiar at least for now.

I needn't have worried; at the end of the summer term in 2012, I was officially given a contract to work with the boy I was currently supporting two afternoons a week in year five on a one-to-one basis in 2012–2013, just in the mornings and with the same teacher as before. I knew that we worked well together and so had no worries about it and looked forward to enjoying my summer holidays, knowing I had a secure job to go back to.

Quite a number of staff were moving at the end of that term; at the leavers' assembly we had to say goodbye not only to our year-six children but also to our deputy head, the infants' teacher who had originally interviewed me when I first went to work at St Paul's, a year-five teacher whom I had supported on Tuesdays and Thursday afternoons with Trent that term, Stuart's teacher, and a new teaching assistant at St Paul's who had suddenly revealed right in the last week of term that she was also moving on. This interested me, as it was she who had taken the job I had interviewed badly for the previous year, and I had already asked the head if there might be a full-time opportunity for me, and he had said that if one came up, he would consider me for the opportunity, and maybe, just maybe, here it was.

We had already interviewed and chosen a new head teacher, and until he had his feet under the table, I felt he would be keeping staffing just as it was. We had all discussed our job prospects all term; many people felt that St Paul's had a lot of teaching assistants, far more than any other school in the locality, and that a new head would want to cut down to save money, so with that slight worry, I was pleased to have been given another one-to-one post, as I felt that that kind of position was far stronger than that of a general intervention TA, as I was at the moment.

CHAPTER 29

TRENT

I had been working with Trent on Tuesday and Thursday afternoons for a while, so I knew what sort of lad he was: highly strung, emotional, and prone to outbursts of temper when he thought things were going against him. The other TAs were having a laugh at my expense, saying that I wouldn't last five minutes with him in the more structured morning sessions; I thought that was a bit much but kept my head down, getting to know him, and waited to see how things panned out.

At the teacher training day on the first day of the new term after the summer holidays, we were asked to bring gardening gloves to help clear the grounds of the weeds that had sprang up over the wet and warm holiday, but on arrival we could see that the weeding had been done. (The head said that the caretaker had been very offended at the thought of the staff doing it, so he had been in all weekend before and done it himself.) We cleared out the art and stationery cupboard instead; all thirty of us formed a long chain to empty it, sort the paper and card into piles, and then restock it.

Whilst doing this quite boring task, most people were chatting about their new charges and still laughing about Trent and the fact I had been appointed to work with him; he hadn't actually got a statement of any sort, and the head was sticking his neck by out employing me to work with him. It was a last-ditch effort to help the teacher work with the new year sixes and year fives in his class. Trent's habit of continually calling out and wanting to talk to the teacher about all sorts of little things but each time turning it into a long-winded conversation from which he couldn't be steered away had wasted a lot of time the previous year and infuriated his teacher. The TAs were getting nowhere trying to deter him from distracting the whole class from what they were meant to be doing, and it had become a habit of the class to visibly relax if someone could tempt Trent into going into one of his stints. I was to try to train him out of it as soon as I could ... Funny how I always get the child no one else wants!!

The first week started reasonably enough; Trent was full of his holidays and wanted to tell anyone who would listen. He didn't like me continually bringing him back on task and saying that he couldn't talk about it now, but he was good natured enough and liked having me all to himself. I did explain that I would be nagging him all the time, as I needed him to be on task and not chattering, but I also explained that I wasn't being mean; I was helping him to get the most out of his last year with us at St Paul's. He was amused by that but didn't mind and started to listen to me quite quickly.

The first morning was going well. I had been with Trent in class until assembly at 10.15 a.m., when I had my break. When I went to find him afterwards for his playtime, I couldn't see him, and I was soon asked to cover the quiet area of the playground outside instead, so I left him to it. But I found him as soon as playtime ended, as I could hear his anguished wails of "I am *so* upset; I *need* to see the head!" I came across him inside in the corridor with the TA who had been watching over the inside play areas. Trent had been playing with Beyblades in a small classroom with a group of boys, and another boy had irritated him; Trent was shouting that he *had* to talk to the head about Derek, the boy who had caused his problem. The TA was trying to calm him down and was speaking to him as though he were about five years old.

I went and stood close by him, but he ignored me. (I felt he was enjoying the fuss and didn't want me to talk him around.) The head obviously heard the commotion, because he left his room and came to see what was happening. He was quick to ignore Trent's protests of unfairness and just quietly said, "How do you feel, Trent? Are you cross, Trent? How cross are you, Trent?" When Trent said that he was "cross enough to swear", the head said, "But you won't swear, will you Trent, because I'll send you home if you do … Tell you what, Trent—are you furious? Can you spell 'furious'? It's f-u-r and then i-o-u-s. What about 'curious'? That's c-u-r and then i-o-u-s."

Trent calmed down enough to listen to him and to stop trying to explain what had happened. Once he'd calmed down enough to complain sensibly about Derek, the head said, "Well, that's easy. Derek isn't playing Beyblades tomorrow, OK, Trent?"

Trent said, "Weeeell, he *can* play, but he has to say sorry," but the head ignored him and told him to use "furious" and "curious" in his writing that day, and that was that. Trent was calm and came back into class wanting to tell his teacher all about it, but I didn't let him; I made him sit down quietly and listen to the rest of the lesson plan that his teacher was explaining to the class. We hadn't missed too much, so I could see what was expected of Trent. Once he got going on the work, he was fine and forgot all about it.

The next day, I was ready for him and took him out of the classroom immediately and sat him down on a sofa in the corridor, and I gave him a foam fist to squeeze in the classroom when he felt like bursting, which he was pleased with. After the previous day's outburst, his teacher had said I was to take Trent out of the class every morning to allow him to have a good start with the class, and it worked very well. Once we were back in class, we sat on a table for two rather than disturb his group, and I worked with him on our own. Every morning thereafter, we did that, and we were always back in class in time for literacy, and Trent was calm sitting with me.

After my break that day, I went to find him before the end of playtime, and in the small classroom where Trent was trying to play with the BeyBlades (spinning toys), Derek was again dancing around, being silly, trying to set Trent off (and beginning to succeed), and so I promptly— and much to his surprise—sent Derek outside and then finished the club for everyone else straight away. Trent was fine and then had the rest of a good morning with me. In literacy the other children did their best to set him off again; when he asked me how to spell "mister" (they were writing informal postcards to pen friends about their holidays or formal letters to a company), Ryan openly scoffed and said, "It's only two letters, m and r, Trent", and that got the other children laughing at him too. But I was right behind Ryan and told him off, which surprised him; he had been talking quietly, but I had heard him loud and clear.

At the same moment, another boy, who had done particularly well, was being moved up the star learner board by the teacher and was basking in the glory while everyone was clapping, but I watched him as he deliberately and smugly made the "loser" sign towards Trent, knowing that the teacher's back was turned. He was very shocked when I immediately went across to the board and moved him back down the board. (The teacher didn't mind at all.) Trent was at first very angry but then immediately calmed when he saw that I had noticed and had treated Harry fairly for his meanness; he wasn't about to get away with that. The other children began to treat me with more respect too, and I felt I was getting to the bottom of Trent's outbursts.

The next week started well, with Trent beginning to trust me to help him to contain his anger and let it out more appropriately (by squeezing his foam fist, silently screaming, etc.), but on the Tuesday I awoke with a splitting headache and stomach ache, and I ended up taking three days off owing to headache and sickness, which was most unpleasant. I went back in on the Friday to hear that Trent had reverted to screaming and shouting and being taken to the quiet room, and therefore not doing any work. He was OK on the Friday, as I immediately started our routine and took him out, and then we were back for literacy as before.

I continued with my quiet support and was soon able to tell quite easily when the other children were trying to wind Trent up, which was so easy for them to do. As well as beginning to help him to understand who his good friends actually were, and who were definitely *not* his friends (which he found very confusing), I was able to see which situations were bearable for Trent and which were not.

During the second week, the children's homework books were due in; they had been handed out on the first Tuesday during literacy and maths, but Trent hadn't been in class at that moment, and no one had told me about them when I had returned from my bout of sickness. It was an unpleasant shock to discover that he was meant to have completed a sheet for literacy and another for maths, as well as have learned ten spellings during the week at home. He had conveniently forgotten to tell me, and I hadn't realised so I hadn't reminded him at all. Of course, he immediately flew into a rage on the Tuesday morning when his teacher announced that he wanted homework in today, shouting, "Well, that's just *great*, that is … I haven't done any homework; no one told me to do any homework …" and he stormed out of the room, on his way home. It took me twenty minutes to calm him down, but he wasn't the only child who hadn't done any homework by a long way (it was a new school year for the children and all routines had been forgotten), and eventually he was mollified enough to come and join in the end of the literacy lesson.

After a pleasant playtime, the exact same thing happened in maths; homework was due in, and he hadn't done any. The maths teacher was very annoyed and told the children who hadn't brought it in that they were to go and see her at lunchtime, which caused another outburst of angry tears from Trent. We had to leave the room again, as the teacher couldn't teach with the noise he was making, and we got nowhere that day at all. It was frustrating and unpleasant, but I was starting to see that Trent wasn't really out of control during his outbursts; he was watching me and gauging my reaction to his behaviour, and he was surprised when I didn't shout at him or insist that he do as he was told just because I said so. He expected me to say that it was OK and that he needn't do any homework if it was going to upset him so, and he was annoyed when, after he'd calmed down again, I said that he must do his homework for the teachers and that he would be doing it during his lunch breaks that week until it was all done. And he would also have more homework to take home and do at home for that week as well; he was going to be busy!

In fact, when I saw him the next day, he had been to see and negotiated with his teachers, and he had got himself a place in Homework Club on Thursday mornings before school, and he was intending to do it all there instead of at home, which I thought was a great idea. That first week, he had to do twice as much as everyone else, but with a teacher to himself to help him, he managed it, and there was no more trouble about not having done it at home, which pleased everyone.

Derek continued to try to wind Trent up; in maths he would throw pens at him, swing on his chair laughing at him, or, if he was in front of us, lean back so far that he was in Trent's way and able to "accidently" brush Trent's papers to the floor. I taught Trent to hold up his hand towards Derek ("talk to the hand") to stop the eye contact, which frustrated Derek but had the desired effect of calming Trent down.

On the Friday of that week, Trent had his first French lesson, which was interesting. I found that he *hated* French and kept repeating loudly that he couldn't do French because "the *French* had sold *Exocets* to the *Argies* in 1982." He said this over and over in such a voice that suggested we had no business trying to teach him such a foul language! It was obviously something he had heard, probably from his dad, and he just wouldn't entertain doing any French. I ignored him completely, and to my surprise, after a while he gave up and found that the lesson was actually quite fun. The children had jigsaw pieces with French and English colours and numbers on them, and to my surprise again, he soon started helping his group to complete their jigsaw and he stopped his chanting. It was a familiar routine on Fridays; he would start up again each time he had French, but he soon forgot about it if no one reacted, and he did the lesson anyway.

Early the next week, we had settled into our routine of going out to read for twenty minutes and then going back into class for literacy. On the Tuesday morning, we went in as usual, but Trent immediately stiffened and turned back around and left the room, absolutely furious. I asked him what the matter was and found he was shaking with rage. He said, "*What* is *she* doing in there? I'm not going back in there if *she's* going to be in there!" I hadn't a clue what he was talking about, but he said that a girl was sitting on the table where he should have been—that is, in the seat that had been his before we started going out of the room. I had to look through the door to see that there was indeed someone in his place, but I didn't recognize who it was from behind.

I did actually know this child a little bit, as I had helped her brother Daniel a few times during the previous term at break times, since he was deeply unpopular with the other children in year six that year and needed the protection of an adult when he was outside during break times, though nobody seemed to know why. Trent said, perversely, that he had liked Daniel, that he thought he was "OK", and that Daniel had given him a Beyblade when he left last term. Actually, he had given it to his sister to give to Trent, and she had done so. I thought that she was probably OK, but Trent said she was a b——, which I thought was unpleasant, and I made sure he didn't repeat that comment anywhere in school. She seemed to suddenly appear in most of Trent's lessons that week; I thought that she had probably been moved down to the lowest group in literacy and maths, since it was unlikely that Trent would have been in a higher group for her to have moved up into, but I didn't know which groups Trent was in, so those were just my musings.

Once she started appearing in maths and literacy, we had another problem to contend with, as well as trying to keep up with the lessons. She regularly sat herself on a back table, level with Trent and me, and she kept staring at Trent, much to his annoyance. I had to teach him a strategy to deal with her. I taught him to hold up his hand if he didn't want to see her looking at him, as he had done with Derek, so that he couldn't see her eyes. I also had him think to himself, "Talk to the hand ... Talk to the hand ..." After a while, the teachers noticed and moved her to the front of the class. They were delighted that Trent was dealing with her without being nasty in any way.

One morning when Trent and I were seated reading on the sofa in the corridor, the head walked past and in his usual way called out, "Morning, Mrs Patrick; Morning, Trent." As Trent opened his mouth to call back, the head calmly put up his palm as if to say, "Talk to the hand" and swept on past on his way somewhere. I said to Trent, "Look, even the head uses that gesture to stop someone talking to him, and it isn't rude, just effective!" I was so pleased; it was almost as though I had asked him to reassure Trent that that was an appropriate way to deal with people he didn't want to see or talk to, but I really hadn't.

The SENCO had only one thing to say about Trent, and that was the problem of him wanting to be too close to his helpers; he leaned against us and cuddled up after he'd been upset, and we needed to stop him being too touchy-feely, as it wasn't appropriate at school or with adults who were not members of his family. Her idea was to buy a soft toy that he could cuddle instead, and she told me to buy something appropriate, up to the value of about £10. Trent said he'd like a dog or a teddy bear, so I had a look at the shops on Saturday and found a perfect little toy—a meerkat with beans at the bottom so he sat upright and alert, but was really soft and cuddly too—and it cost £7.99. We named him "Mikey", and Trent loved him straight away. He lived in my bag during the mornings and in a cupboard over lunchtime to be ready for his afternoon helper if he was needed then too, and he came out for a cuddle whenever Trent needed one.

Trent's individual education plan (IEP) meeting was scheduled for a Wednesday afternoon the next week, so I had a school dinner that day and stayed for the meeting. We started late, as the previous parent had taken a long time in their meeting, but I had met Trent's mum in the corridor while we were both waiting, and we had chatted pleasantly enough. Trent was so like his mother; it was quite obvious why he was like he was. She talked incessantly about nothing at all, just to talk rather than be silent, and she was incredibly angry whenever she mentioned Trent's father. I was pleased to get away from it when we went into the meeting room. She told us that she had an appointment for Trent the next day with an educational psychologist to try to get him a statement of special educational needs (SEN), which the school wanted as well, as they had taken a big risk employing me to work on a one-to-one basis with Trent even though there was no money coming in for him to cover my salary; a statement of SEN would provide the money to pay me. Trent's teacher and our SENCO spent the meeting telling his mum just how much it was helping Trent to have me there each day; his literacy and maths work was vastly improved, and his general behaviour was so much calmer. Everyone was delighted, and the head, his teacher, and the SENCO all said that the reason was simply having me there, and they complimented me on my fabulous progress with Trent. I was delighted.

The other TAs in school were by now also commenting on how much better Trent was and grudgingly congratulating me for doing what none of them had managed in the previous years with him. I wished I knew what it was that I was doing so differently to them, but the only difference I could easily see was that they treated children in a very babyish and angry way when the children behaved badly, whilst I was always calm and respectful towards my children. I expected good behaviour and usually got it, and the children with me had to decide to work and behave well for themselves, not just for me. It was the children who lost out if they lost playtime or treats through their own behavioural outbursts, and I helped them to see that, as well as letting them see that if they did well and the teachers rewarded them, then it was themselves that they could be proud of, rather than thinking that they had just done as they were told. When they got it right, it was because they had learned the right way to behave, and it was not just chance that the teacher had been pleased with them.

The day that Trent had his appointment out of school, I was placed with Cameron in the next classroom, as his TA was off ill that day. He grudgingly, and with much prompting, wrote his diary entry, although he told me he didn't usually have to do it. I hadn't been advised of that, so I ignored his protests. He then worked well in literacy and again in maths with me, and afterwards it was all round the school—whispers of "Did you see how much Cameron wrote?" and "Wow, he was actually in maths today!" When he had had his spelling test just before lunch (having cheekily told me that he hadn't practised so would rather go and play hockey as usual instead—no chance!) and had tried to spell all of his words with varying success and I had then marked all of his table's work as well as his, even the teacher had commented that she wished all the TAs were like me!

Sometimes I honestly wonder what other TAs actually *do* in school. All I had had to do was note where he was on the learning board when I first arrived, tell him where he was, and then tell him that I was keeping track of how much he was working. If he was off task, I would start counting down on my fingers from five to one. When I got to one, I would simply tell him that he was going down the board, and then I only had to silently move my finger up and down my other hand, counting, to remind him all morning, and he was then no problem at all.

When I arrived at school the following Monday, the head took me aside to explain that another senior member of staff had announced that she was leaving us at Christmas. The acting deputy head would be leaving, after the loss of the deputy head in September, as she had just got married and had secured a post at a school nearer to where she lived with her new husband. This was quite disturbing; with the loss of all our most senior members of staff, things were going to be very different in January.

Time with Trent was becoming very tiring; he allowed anything to upset his mornings and took longer and longer to recover. The next Tuesday was a case in point; Trent had come in a little late and the children he was coming in with took a shortcut through a fence in the playground, and Trent said that he was shouted at even though he'd been the only one who hadn't gone through the fence. I hadn't seen the incident, but I explained to Trent that sometimes teachers get it wrong, that no one tries to be nasty to him in particular, and that he had been unlucky that time. The teacher who had shouted was the one who was leaving, so I told Trent that I thought she wasn't feeling very well that day and that we all make mistakes. He finally allowed himself to be mollified, and with the promise of a cuddle with Mikey, he managed to come into class and got on with his morning.

The week ploughed on with Trent becoming more and more belligerent, and by Friday I had had enough; I had been fighting off a cold all the week and feeling less and less able to cope, and on Friday I awoke with such a sore throat and headache that I called in sick. I was unwell all the weekend and continued to feel awful for all of Monday and Tuesday. On Wednesday I went in, feeling a little better, to find that lots of staff members were also off with the same sore throat and headache, and that I was the first one back. I always felt bad taking time off, but when I was not on top form, I could not cope with whomever it was I was working with, and I often felt that I would be doing more harm than good if I ploughed on, not coping and allowing the child to get the upper hand. We had only three more days until half term, and Trent was obviously not looking forward to it; his behaviour was very unsettled, and he was easily upset.

On Thursday we entered the classroom in the morning to find Trent's things had been scattered around the classroom, and he understandably went ballistic. Someone had been in his tray again and messed his stuff up. While I was away earlier in the week, someone had taken his reading book from his tray, and it had vanished, which was frustrating, as there wasn't another copy that he could read instead. It took me, another TA, *and* another teacher to calm him down this time; the teacher went into the class and read the riot act to the rest of the children while Trent and I were out of the room, which mollified Trent so he could carry on with his day at school. Friday was OK, but we were all glad it was half term!

My husband had also taken the half-term week off work, but he was very tired and started vomiting on Sunday, so it wasn't all that restful a weekend after all. I started back to work on the first Monday after half term but was still feeling unwell, and on Tuesday I went to the doctor to find that I was suffering with something called pharyngitis. All I knew was that my throat was very sore and that I was exhausted. I took the next five days off on a self-certificate, and then on the Monday I went to the doctor again and was signed off for a further week and given antibiotics. The next weekend, I started to feel better and went into work on the Monday, but by the afternoon I was feeling worse, so I again saw the doctor and was signed off for another week, and then for yet another week with another bout of different antibiotics to try to get rid of the infection. I was feeling pretty wretched and so fed up with the whole thing. On the plus side, though, I managed to make up a batch of scarves for Christmas presents whilst I was sitting quietly in the warm! I ended up taking six weeks off suffering with what turned out to be gastro-oesophageal reflux and had to start a new medication to control the acid in my stomach, which had burned my throat badly. I was off for the entire half term and went back after Christmas.

Trent was very pleased to see me when we started back, although he was quite difficult during the first few weeks, as he had to sit a lot of practice SATs papers, and he hates those. I managed to get him to at least try by telling him that it made his teacher look like a very bad teacher if his pupils couldn't manage their SATs, and as Trent liked him, he did try.

I had one occasion when I was called back from my morning break as Trent was having a meltdown in the corridor. Natasha, another TA, had tried to intervene when Trent had been teased by another child; he had left the room as we always had him do if the alternative was to thump somebody, and Natasha had told him he was going to lose his break if he didn't go straight back into class. Naturally he was outraged and wouldn't go back in, so she had told him he had lost his lunch break free time too, and he had totally lost it. His teacher had come to get me, but by the time I arrived, Trent had totally gone past the point of no return and Natasha was rather smug in her assessment of the situation; she had dished out a punishment, and I had to deal with the fallout.

In her opinion, Trent was unreachable, and I was wasting my time trying to help him cope with school. I went to the quiet room where Trent had been taken, and he proceeded to kick the walls and throw his shoes about and scream and cry uncontrollably; I sat in the middle of the room and waited for him to calm a little. Once he was lying on a beanbag, sobbing, I took out a piece of bubble wrap that I always keep in my bag and asked him what had happened. As he told me that another boy had teased him, I snapped some bubbles, saying that it made me feel better and that I was cross with that boy for being unfair. Trent eyed the bubble wrap and asked if he could have it, so I passed it across, and he snapped bubbles and then wrung the plastic in his hands as if he were strangling it, producing a most satisfying loud popping noise. By now he was smiling. I started drawing on my pad of paper, and he joined in. We drew a space scene with rockets and stars and planets, and I was able to talk quietly to him about what had happened. I explained that I understood his frustration, but that Natasha's decision had to stand, and he would indeed lose both breaks.

By that time, it was time for maths anyway, and he had already missed morning break. Trent managed maths very well, and afterwards he said he wanted to apologise to Natasha and see if she would relent about lunch break. I said she wouldn't, but we saw her on the way back to his class, and he rushed over to ask her. She said that she would like to relent, as he had apologised but that she couldn't, and her decision stood. She then asked me to keep him out of the way over lunchtime, as she couldn't have him having a temper tantrum on the playground, but I said that I had Stuart at lunchtime and that she would have to have Trent on the playground. She realised her mistake then, but it was too late, and I left her to deal with it, silly woman.

I got very tired of Natasha throwing her weight about regarding Trent. She could see that I could cope with him and indeed get very good behaviour and quality work out of him, and she couldn't stand to see it.

We had a good few weeks after that with no outbursts—at least not in the mornings when I was there. He was always unhappy after any weekend that had included seeing his dad. I learned just before half term that Trent's afternoon carer was leaving, as she had a new job nearer home; I felt that this was extremely selfish and so unsettling for Trent, and then he was off sick for the last two days of the half term, so he didn't even get to say goodbye to her. I wasn't looking forward to his reaction after half term! I did offer to stay all day for the next half term, since it was a very short one with only four weeks until Easter, but the Key Stage 2 leader said she wanted to see how he was without support, at least for a while.

Half term came, and with it a bout of flu, so I was miserable in myself but buoyant because my husband and son had had such good news the week before. Charles had applied to five universities and had been asked to interview at them all, and after three of the interviews, he had three offers. His favourite, Teesside, had offered him a bursary of £2,000 to go there, and since he was planning to anyway—and to house-share with his friend Gabriel from college, whose mum had already bought them a small house to rent ten minutes' walk away from the university—he couldn't have been happier. Nigel had also been interviewed, this time for promotion, and we heard on the Friday that he had been promoted! He was now a captain with the Royal Fleet Auxiliary; we were all so proud!

The next part of the term was only four weeks long, as Easter was so early, and it passed very quickly indeed. Trent was becoming very touchy about being asked which school he was to go to next year; I discovered why at a teacher training day when we had a day of Team Teach training. I got to talk to our SENCO, and she said that Trent's mum had failed to get his application in on time and so he hadn't received an offer of a place at any school yet, and it was looking increasingly unlikely that he would get his first choice of North Leamington School. This was almost the only topic of discussion with the other children, and so it alienated Trent even more. He did eventually get his place confirmed at North Leam and seemed pleased that a few of his classmates were also going there. The next term brought with it the SATs mock papers, and Trent had meltdown after meltdown; it was a really trying time for all of us. He managed a few papers but nearly always ended up screwing them up and screaming with frustration.

My mum began to be unwell about this time, and I started taking her to hospital appointments and doctor's appointments most weeks, usually managing to arrange them during the afternoons so I didn't have to have much time off work. It was so much better having her very local to me; I was able to pop in every day and to help her shower and make sure she was taking her medication properly. She was beginning to get confused over lots of things, and the medication was quite complicated, with different pills on different days and one of them being soluble (needing to be dissolved in water), along with constipation remedies with all the graphic descriptions that I could have done without! I had to assume all responsibility for her, which ate up even more of my time, but I felt privileged to be able to help her so much; I knew that I wouldn't have her for very much longer and was enjoying spending time with her every day.

Trent progressed into the actual SATs week with surprising enthusiasm, and I had high hopes for his attempts. On the Monday, his first SAT was an English one, which was incredibly difficult, and he had a couple of meltdowns. I was able to take him outside to cool off, but he ended up having to speak with the head and didn't manage to finish the paper, which was a shame.

I was dreading the next day, but it was OK. The paper was another English one; this time it involved grammar and punctuation, which he managed fine. The next two days he sailed through, as he enjoys maths.

He managed first the "no calculator" one and then the "calculator allowed" one with no problems at all.

On the Thursday of SATs week, once they had finished their SATs and breathed a collective sigh of relief, the children were informed that they were going to be putting on an end-of-term year six play. They didn't know what it was going to be, but they had to say whether they wanted a main part or a small part and whether or not they were prepared to sing and dance. Trent asked for a main part, and then on the Friday, they spent the morning watching a play in the hall. It was *Oliver Twist*, and the children were buzzing with excitement, as that was the play they were going to perform. Trent decided that he wanted to be the Artful Dodger and made sure everyone knew it, so when the parts were allocated that afternoon he was disgusted to be given the part of Mr Brownlow, and he spent an hour screaming and shouting that he didn't want to be in the stupid play. He calmed down eventually when I didn't react and didn't say that he had to be in it; I let him let all the frustration out and then said that if he still felt the same at the end of the day, we would give his part to someone else.

By the Monday, he had got used to the idea and began to be excited too. The children were to spend the next seven weeks (their last weeks at primary school) looking at all aspects of *Oliver Twist*. They wrote biographies of Charles Dickens and designed book covers in the first week, along with starting to read through the play script.

As the weeks progressed, the play began to take shape. The children with main parts did very well and learnt their lines quickly, the songs were practised over and over again, and the other TAs and I made props and backdrops whenever we had chance. Many of the children were not in the right frame of mind, and so we had to start a "zero-tolerance" list and added to it each day, with offenders not being allowed to play 40/40 in the free time sessions—not that they really cared. Trent was occasionally on this list, and he did care; he made a lot of fuss, but the rules were the same for everybody, and he had to miss his fair share of the games too. However, he knew his lines and was doing well. The show went very well, with all of them at their best on the night of the performance.

CHAPTER 30

DANIEL

The following school year, I was given the role of general teaching assistant, again in the same class, year five/six, but I was also spending some time individually with a child in year six—an 11-year-old called Daniel. At the start of the school year, he was excluded for his atrocious behaviour; I had noticed him during the previous year having stand-up arguments with lots of teachers, and I was quite pleased not to be working with him myself at that time. He had an outside support worker in school, but nothing seemed to help. He was forever coming in for a trial day and going home in disgrace again, time after time after time.

Just before Christmas, I was asked if I would work with him in the spring term 2014. I had reservations and said that I didn't want to be one-to-one with Daniel; he was a very big lad—the same height as me! With his aggression and constant arguing, I wasn't sure that I could help him or that I would feel safe working with him. It was decided that I would be in the classroom that Daniel was in all the time, but not one-to-one with him specifically. Daniel thought that he was starting a new term without any support; we wanted to see how he would manage without such close supervision but with an adult keeping a close eye on him and intervening where necessary.

To begin with, Daniel was in school only for the morning lessons. He would start in class, but as soon as he started to act up, he would be asked to leave, which he always refused to do, arguing loudly that he didn't see why he should leave the room. He usually ended up swearing at the teacher and telling me to leave him alone. "Are you stalking me?" became his taunt towards me whenever I followed him out of the room. "You're not my support person!" he would shout.

I often had to enlist the help of the head and the deputy head just to get Daniel out of a class, and sometimes we took all the other children away instead to leave Daniel on his own, throwing chairs, overturning tables, and swearing loudly. He really was most unpleasant.

Often he would end up in the blue room that Trent had used, and most days he would then fall asleep on the beanbags. It was obvious to me that a lot of the problem was that Daniel was just plain exhausted. He looked grey and had huge bags under his eyes, he was clumsy and walked into things—he was dead on his feet. I spent many hours sitting outside the blue room while Daniel slept inside. There was no point in trying to talk to him, as I would just be shouted at, so I would state that I could see that he was too tired to do any work and that he should calm down and have a sleep if he needed to. He would sleep for hours! Once it was time to go home, I would gently wake him and snatch a brief chance to talk to him while he was feeling refreshed and not angry.

He just wanted to be like everyone else—in the classroom, being taught. He was very aware that he didn't have much more time in primary school and that no secondary school would take him with his behaviour issues. I wanted him to understand that if he wasn't so tired he would be able to get up and have a decent breakfast before school. He couldn't see the point of eating breakfast (he would usually say "I'm too fat already; I don't want to eat"), but I often let him choose a piece of fruit from the free fruit for schools box, and I would sneak him a couple of digestive biscuits too.

His attitude in the mornings was never great, and his having had a shouting match at home when his mum had tried to get him up in the morning meant he was usually angry too. He arrived late every day, if he came at all, and would kick the playground gate open, much to the fury of the head, as it was getting looser and looser at its hinge on the wall and was becoming dangerous. He would stomp into school to be met by an irate head asking him to stop kicking the gate open. If asked why he did it, he would growl, "'Cos I'm bored!" We didn't often have a good start to the mornings.

He was actually very intelligent and was able to do all of the work set for him. After a while, he spent most of his mornings in the blue room—a calm, cool room to chill out in, where he did his work—but he still resented the fact he wasn't allowed to be with the other children in class. The head's sole aim for the term was to get Daniel prepared for his SATs so he could show what he could do and have a better chance of being accepted at a decent secondary school. The other children in his class lost out because of all the fuss whenever Daniel appeared, as he would needle the teacher until he or she was shouting at him, but he always refused to leave the room.

Quite often he would be marched down to the head's office and made to stand outside in the corridor until the head was free to talk to Daniel. A couple of times whilst standing outside the room, he was mysteriously found lying on the floor, covered with blood from a carpet burn to his face. He went to hospital the first time it happened, because he said he didn't know what had happened; he'd just fallen over and woken up covered with blood. After that I was instructed to shadow him very closely, which he resented even more.

He wasn't allowed to go swimming on Tuesday mornings after that, because the hospital couldn't come up with a reason why he had collapsed, and they said it was too dangerous to allow him to swim. Actually, we all suspected that he had done it on purpose, so revoking his swimming privilege was a good way to call his bluff, and he didn't do it again.

We continued in this way all term, and gradually he allowed me to talk to him and even started smiling and laughing with me. I never put myself in any position where I was alone with him, since I had been warned that he had accused adults of molesting him in the past, and we even sometimes went back to class once he'd calmed down enough.

By the end of the half term after Easter, we were on quite good terms.

He was spending more time in class and leaving when I asked him to; he was then working well in the blue room, and he was very much more alert. His mum reported that he was going to bed when asked to and was getting up in good time too. With SATs looming, I was told he would take them all on his own in the blue room and not in the hall with the other children. The head fully expected him to disrupt the exams and didn't want to give him the chance. Daniel resented it, but to my delight he buckled down and completed every single one. The teachers were as pleasantly surprised as I was!

He then had a few really good weeks and was at last offered the chance to resume coming to school full time for the rest of the term. He was still difficult and tended to swear a lot, but gradually he came around to my way of thinking, and before long we had a great relationship. I could talk to him, reassure him, and coax him to do whatever it was the teacher wanted, and he began to produce startlingly impressive work. He wrote a horror story worthy of publishing and then wrote another about the same character, saying that maybe he would turn them into a book when he was older. He surprised me by saying that when he got it published, he would put me in the credits because I was the one who had motivated him! He then wrote a moving and emotional poem dedicated to a girl he'd known at his previous school but had had to leave behind when he left.

He was offered a place at a special secondary school in Nuneaton on the strength of his ability coupled with his difficulties; he had also received a statement of Asperger's syndrome, which made sure he got his place there.

On his last afternoon at St Paul's, he was quite emotional, saying goodbye to everyone; he even gave me a hug, which was amazing. I gave him a book about getting his stories published (*The Writer's Yearbook*), which he loved. I then walked with him to the bus stop to catch a bus home; his mum had phoned to say that she couldn't collect him and that he was to go home by bus that day. The head wasn't happy about it, but I was able to accompany him, so it was OK.

Daniel had to be the hardest pupil I had tried to help, and also the most satisfying.

Just before the end of the term, the head asked me if I would work with a year-two boy next term, mornings only, so I spent any spare time I had getting to know him whenever Daniel wasn't there. He was a boy I hadn't really come across before, so I wondered what was in store for me in the next year at St Paul's.

CHAPTER 31

TIMMY

Timmy presented as an extremely polite little boy who didn't want to work if he could draw instead, and he wasn't interested in learning to read, write, or understand numeracy.

To begin with, I just concentrated on getting to know him; I found that he was left-handed and would consider a sum only if it was written right to left, but if it was an addition sum, then he would scream, "No! I *hate* God!" and go underneath the table as soon as he saw an addition sign, as he saw it as a cross. Any attempt to see what he understood literacy-wise was met with a grumpy "I just want to draw!" By trial and error, I discovered his favourite obsession—sharks of all kinds, particularly megalodons from the dinosaur period—which trumped all other interests, of which he had many.

He was very knowledgeable about most things to do with nature, I found, and he was delighted when I produced a book that I had found in a bargain bookshop called *8000 Awesome Facts You Should Know*, which had an enormous section on sharks of every description, size, shape, and habit. We began to go to this brilliant book whenever he asked a question about sharks or told me a fact I wanted to corroborate, and we then moved on to looking at the book's contents page so he could choose what he wanted to look up.

When we drew in the mornings, I started to draw sharks using letters to encourage him to form his letters correctly, so we used *o* for eyes, *c* for gills, *v* and *w* for teeth, *u* for the body, and so on. He was fascinated and got really good at it! We then progressed to also using numbers: sixes for eyes, sideways sevens for fins, etc. His teacher was delighted at the progress he quickly made and his obvious pride in his accomplishments.

One of the biggest bugbears for him was morning assembly. He had steadfastly refused to go ever since he had tried it in nursery and reception, and the familiar "I *hate* God!" rang out each and every morning. The teachers had usually given in and allowed him not to go rather than cause a huge fuss, but assembly time was my time to have a break with a cup of coffee in the staff room, and I didn't want to have to miss that every day!

I found that his family were not Christian but Buddhist, and that Timmy came to a church school only because it was the closest to home, so I figured that the most upsetting bit of the assembly was probably likely to be the prayer at the end. I made a deal with him. He was to go into assembly with his class, and I would have a shorter break and collect him before the end each time. This worked immediately! He often commented, "That assembly was really interesting!" as he skipped back to our classroom before the prayers, and he always had his piece of fruit first (his early departure allowing him to select a piece before the crush) and was ready for playtime when the assembly finished just a few minutes later.

At first playtimes were a trial for Timmy. He didn't have any friends, as he was always so grumpy and wouldn't ever share a toy or let anyone else play with it with him. He would just stand sadly on his own, growling at any child who wanted to play with him. He started to play with me when I rolled a hoop for him to chase after and catch, and sometimes other children joined in too.

At the end of break, when the bell went, he would shoot down to the bottom of the playground and hide. I was wearily told by the other adults outside at playtime that he would always refuse to come in after playtime and that I would have to find him and threaten him with sanctions for not doing as he was told. I decided to flip that on its head and watch where he had hidden himself and then turn it into a game. I would wander around "looking" for him, and then I would stop and sniff and say, "Fee fie foe fum, I smell a Timmy having some fun!" He would giggle and burst out with a "Here I am!" and a huge grin. Often we would get into the classroom first as the other children lined up waiting to be taken in; we walked past them all and went in chatting. His teachers were just amazed.

After a few weeks into September I had spent the weekend at a county scout camp with my husband Nigel. We had been running the craft tent for the weekend, and Nigel had used a piece of rainbow scraperfoil to make a multicoloured bookmark for Timmy. It had his name on it, with sharks and a yellow ribbon. It was lovely, and I put it in my bag to take it to school. I forgot all about it until the Wednesday, when I suddenly saw it in my bag right at the end of the morning and gave it to Timmy. He was absolutely delighted! He showed it to his teacher, who suggested he might like to write a thank-you note for Nigel, and bless him, he wanted to! It made him late for lunch, but he carefully wrote in coloured pencil, "Thank you for my marvellous bookmark, Nigel!" and I photocopied it for his evidence book. This was such a breakthrough; it was a real turning point for Timmy.

His teacher asked me to go through some sheets of phonics with him to try to see what he actually knew. They were very dry and boring, just lists of words to decipher for each stage, so we turned it into a game (as usual!). I would write all the words on my whiteboard and challenge Timmy to find each word as I said it, cross it off on my board, and write it on his own. He was able to read every single word on the first three sheets! I delightedly told him that he was reading, and he said, "No I'm not, I can't read! I just look at the first letter and try to sound out the other letters afterwards." I explained that this *was* reading, and that furthermore, because he was able to read each word totally out of context, (i.e., random words that didn't go together), he would find books *much* easier, as they had sentences and pictures to give clues as to what each word might be. He was rather dubious but was ready to have a go.

The next week, he produced his first homework on time with the other children. He had asked to do it at home with his mum's boyfriend, who had been happy to help, and they had written and drawn together and made a wonderful book about superheroes (our theme for the term). This was the first piece of homework that Timmy had *ever* produced.

A few weeks later, he was getting on and joining in and doing his numeracy and literacy and homework as required and didn't really need me, so I was available to help other children. When I had a few days off with a chest infection, his teacher texted me to say that Timmy was also off with a chest infection but that he had been reading for pleasure at home! His mum had photographed him reading and sent the photos in for her to see, and she entered it into the competition and was thrilled to find that Timmy had won the school prize for the most improvement in reading for the term. Even though I felt pretty rotten whilst waiting for the antibiotics to kick in, I couldn't help grinning from ear to ear myself!

(HAPTER 32

MUM

My chest infection got worse, and the doctor diagnosed bronchitis. It didn't clear up, and I had weeks off work, feeling very unwell and very unhappy. My mum was not well either, so I didn't dare go into the home where she was in case I infected everybody, so I went in only a few times over the next few weeks. Mum suddenly took a turn for the worse and was taken into hospital; she was there for thirteen days, very annoyed at being in bed, and saying that she wasn't ill, but the catheter bag of dark brown urine and her low oxygen count told a very different story. My brother Jeremy came over a couple of times to visit her. Nigel was away at sea and wasn't able to help, so it was lovely when Charles came home for the holidays and came to see her each day with me. We went in as usual one afternoon to find her much more unwell than before. She didn't talk to us but held our hands and gazed across the room as if in a daze. The morning after that visit, I got a phone call at 5.50 a.m. to say that she had taken another turn for the worse. I was there within ten minutes, but she had already died. It was 22 December. She was eighty-nine years old and had missed her ninetieth birthday by nine days. It was such a shock, but also a relief as she wasn't suffering any more, and I managed to go into autopilot to make all the necessary arrangements.

I had previously offered to cook Christmas dinner for the whole family, so I carried on with that, and it went very well, and Christmas was a rather muted affair for once, but we got through it. Afterwards, I had thought

I was coping well, but suddenly I wasn't coping at all. I had a flare up of bipolar symptoms and was suddenly very unwell indeed. My medication was dramatically increased, and everything just became a blur. Charles was supposed to go back up to university, but he asked permission to stay at home for a further week to look after me, and he was able to stay, which helped so much. I stayed at home with Charles, coping less and less well. It would have been mum's ninetieth birthday on 31 December, and I contacted the funeral director the day before to say how much I appreciated them looking after her, but they said that they hadn't collected her from the morgue because of the holidays. Realising that she was still basically in a fridge unhinged me completely, and I cried and cried all day and night, with Charles trying to support me. I called our church minister the next day (completely not thinking that it was New Year's Eve), and he came and prayed with me. It suddenly started to snow, but only in the back garden—not in the front. He said, "There's your mum's message; she's arrived!" I felt much comforted.

Once Charles went back to university, the doctor insisted that I either go into a mental hospital or go to stay with family, and Nigel's parents took me in. I stayed with them for about six weeks. I was off work until Easter. I had my driving licence revoked because of the heavy sedation I was under, and I stayed with Nigel's parents until I felt well enough to catch a bus and go home every few days or so. When I was at home, I felt much better, but I had to go back each evening to sleep at their house. It was wonderful of them to support me, but they were both elderly (Jane was eighty-six and Alan ninety), and it was putting quite a strain on all of us. Eventually I was well enough to go home on my own, but without a driving licence, I was still relying on buses to get around.

When I did go back to work, it was on a gradual return basis; I started with just going in for the lunch-hour playtime, and then I gradually added one morning a week, going in by bus. By half term I was back up to my usual hours and feeling a lot better about everything.

Timmy had managed magnificently without me, and he had a surprise for me when I got back—he was reading and writing fluently! His dad had been working with him a lot, as he home-schooled Timmy's older sister, and it had really paid off; I was so delighted for him.

When the summer holidays came around, I was much better, and I got my driving licence back the day before we went on holiday. Nigel and I went to Australia for three weeks, followed by six days in New Zealand and three days in Bangkok. It was the holiday of a lifetime, for which we had saved up for months to go in this special year, 2015, the year of our thirtieth wedding anniversary and my fiftieth birthday. We had a wonderful time; I met my half-sister Gail in Perth and my friend and past colleague Amanda in New Zealand, and there was a lot of time for Nigel and I to talk and reconnect properly, and we came home refreshed and much happier all round. Nigel had to go back to sea almost straight away, but I had a further two weeks of holiday, and Charles was still at home for three weeks after we got home. Charles and I took Nigel to Heathrow Airport. I went back to work, and a week later I drove Charles to Cardiff to start his year's internship with a computer games company in Cardiff. I was completely on my own again but feeling fine and soon loving being back at work.

CHAPTER 33

JACK

My new charge was a boy in year three, whom I supervised along with a teacher new to the school. I had been spending a little time with him during the previous term to try to get to know him while he was in year two. He was a boy with a temper who often snapped over little things and completely went off the rails; he spent a lot of time calming down in the blue room. I could see that I was going to have a lot of trouble with him, as he didn't seem to me to be autistic, which I was used to; it seemed to me that he was just badly behaved, very rude, and often violent if he didn't get his own way. I met his mum, and when she learned that I was to be his new support worker, she just shook her head and said, "Good luck!"

The first week went well. Jack and Timmy were in the same class, and the other teaching assistant in the class was Jack's previous support worker, and so although I was supposed to be with Jack, and she with Timmy, the boys naturally came to the adult they were used to and all was well. The second week got trickier as we gradually weaned the boys off the wrong adult and tried to work with our own charges, but Jack hated having me trailing after him, and Timmy objected to having a new adult around him. The first PE lesson went well enough, but after the second PE lesson of the week, Timmy refused to change back into his uniform, as it wasn't named, and he was certain it wasn't his. The teacher wasn't there at the time, and I eventually managed to get him to dress after twenty minutes with the help of a wasp that conveniently buzzed into our room; I told Timmy that it would ignore him if he had his clothes on, and that worked!

Meanwhile, Jack was starting to try it on and just getting up to leave the room whenever he felt like it, and then running all over the school trying to get me to go away. I never chased after him; I knew he couldn't get out of school, and I made sure that I had something interesting to do while I waited for him to come back, which he always did!

It didn't seem all that long before Jack settled with me. We spent a lot of time in the blue room at first, but eventually he was managing fine in class and began to get really good at literacy and numeracy with my constant support and encouragement. After only one term, I was asked if I would support a different child in the same classroom, as Jack didn't really need me anymore. I often said that I felt like Nanny McFee; the child I was assigned to never wanted me and was full of resentment at first, but once he or she settled and started to like having me around, I would move on!

CHAPTER 34

SAM

Sam was another boy in my usual class. He was extremely anxious and never came into school without a huge fuss. He would have to be taken to the blue room by two adults once his mum had finally managed to force him through the front door, and then he would scream and crash around the room for over an hour before he calmed down. Very occasionally his mum would manage to get him round to the playground with all of the other children in juniors before school, but then he would refuse to come into school at all.

The head began to insist that his mum take him to the blue room if he wouldn't let her leave, so that the onus was more on her getting him to settle than on us. More often than not, he would cling to his mum in the blue room and cry and beg her not to leave him for over an hour each morning while she looked at me and mouthed, "What do I do?" It was so distressing for both of them, but at least it took only me out of circulation instead of two other members of staff, and it gave me chance to begin to get to know him better.

His younger brother would come into school like anyone else and calmly go off to his own classroom; indeed, we tried not to allow Sam to get to his climax of screaming while Luke was watching. They were totally different personalities, which added fuel to our argument that Sam's behaviour was learnt and not due to autism as his mother was insisting.

At first I had to watch helplessly while he was being forced into the blue room and then feel impotent and unable to help while he was out of control. He would suddenly flip, though, and become happy and smiling, shake himself down, and calmly go to class as though nothing had happened. His behaviour in class was another matter. Within minutes he would be rolling around on the floor, playing at dinosaurs and totally disrupting the class, at which point I would be asked to remove him. If I could persuade him to leave the room with me, I had nothing for him to do except use an iPad to calm him down by playing with some of the games on there. It wasn't ideal, since he was learning nothing at all, but the teachers all said the same thing: "Take him away!"

Eventually I managed to get his teacher to show me the work he was supposed to be doing, and we would talk about it outside in the corridor. I started getting him to copy some writing into his handwriting book each morning with the promise of iPad time afterwards, and I talked to him about anything and everything. I would write something in his book that was positive for him to copy, and he began doing that every day. Soon his book was full of amazing writing, really neat and carefully done, and he began to show real pride in it.

I was able to start introducing his classwork for him to complete with me outside the classroom, and while it wasn't as good as his handwriting and was mostly me suggesting things that he could write about in his books, he soon began to enjoy that too. It was obvious that he had an anxiety disorder of some sort, but gradually he began to come into school more calmly, giving Mum a kiss and letting her go to work. We were getting his work done too, so his teacher wasn't as exasperated as she had been.

We filled in some forms for an educational psychologist about him, as we were wondering whether he had pathological demand avoidance (PDA), and just kept going as best we could whilst awaiting her verdict. It made some sort of sense to me, as the paperwork on PDA that I was given suggested that a coping method of these children was to appear to give in and to comply, but only when given two choices of what to do. So rather than insisting he do his work (flat refusal was always the answer to that one!), I would give him a choice of two pieces of work so he could choose one without being told to do it, and that worked well. On the outside, it looked as though Sam had settled and was working well for me, but it was so difficult keeping up the act of allowing him choice and keeping him calm when most of the adults in school were upset with him after years of bad behaviour for them. I was enjoying the challenge and pleased with the results so far, but I was also getting quite anxious and depressed myself now that Nigel had gone back to sea and I was on my own at home for long periods of time.

Eventually a place was found for Sam at a special school fairly nearby; he had to go by taxi each day but appeared to be thriving at last. I continued in Sam's class after he had left, helping wherever I could. I was then asked to go down to infants to work with a child called Ned.

CHAPTER 35

NED

Ned was a 6-year-old autistic boy in year two, and he was in Sam's younger brother's class. Luke was a difficult child too and appeared to be trying to copy his brother Sam in an attempt to be able to leave. However, as he and Ned were friends, I was able to work with them both together, and Luke settled, as did Ned. I worked with Ned for the rest of that school year and then went with him into year three, which took him into juniors at school. As had so often happened with lots of children before, just being in year three meant that Ned grew up suddenly and barely needed me.

Ned's dad always brought him to school, and he came in each day quite happily. They would be deep in conversation, and Ned never acknowledged my cheery "Good morning, Ned," but his dad always did. His dad was enormous—a bodybuilder with a very deep voice and always very friendly. His mum came in occasionally to see an assembly or concert that Ned was in, but she never came on her own. I learned much later that she had multiple sclerosis. Ned's dad told me this on one occasion when Ned needed to go home with an upset tummy and his dad couldn't come, so I had suggested mum might. He said that she never left the house on her own because of her illness. When I mentioned this to our SENCO, she said it had never been mentioned, and so I began to doubt what Ned's dad said. He was very controlling, and I felt that there was some sort of abuse going on but could never pinpoint anything.

Ned had a younger brother who was also autistic, and he was mute. He went to a special school in the next town, as his needs were more complex than Ned's. Ned was able to read very well, but his writing was illegible and his pencil grip very awkward. He would fly into a rage over nothing, and he didn't have many friends.

Eating was a huge deal for him; he never had any fruit at break time, and lunch was an isolated affair where he would sit with me in an otherwise empty room and pick at his lunch. He always had a cheese sandwich, which had to be on the right sort of bread or else he wouldn't touch it. With that he would have a fruit roll (a sweet, sugary snack), a pack of Cheese strings and a packet of Quavers or Pom-Bear crisps. It was a very bland lunch, and he often said he was full before he had eaten anything!

With perseverance I managed eventually to get him to eat his lunch in the dining hall; this was a huge step forward. He began to make more friends, and year three was amazing for him. He managed, with support, to sit on the carpet with the rest of the children for group lessons. After a while, he learnt that I always stood in the same place at outside break times so that he could find me if he needed me quickly. I kept my eye on him throughout break, and I would move my feet to point to him so I could see quickly if he went anywhere else in the playground. This foot system worked very well; I knew just where he was, and he knew where I was, so I could just let him play without too obviously shadowing him.

Unfortunately, I didn't manage to see Ned through the whole school year, as I had an unexpected bipolar episode.

CHAPTER 36

HOSPITAL

I had another major bipolar episode in November 2017, which came completely out of the blue. I had been beginning to slide upwards in my mood, and I was becoming more loudly spoken at work and feeling overconfident.

Nigel was working in the UK for a while, which involved him travelling from Portsmouth to Liverpool for a course one week. On the way back, he popped in for coffee. It was great to have him back, and I didn't want him to go, as I was feeling very unwell in my mood and I was worried that I might have another episode. Nigel dismissed my worries and went back to Portsmouth anyway.

I very quickly deteriorated and found myself calling the police to accuse my brother of sexual abuse and to tell them I was worried that he might still be abusing little girls. I had heard from his wife that he had left them months earlier, which I had had no idea about. I knew now that he had a lot of money, as his wife's new boyfriend had given him half of the value of their house so she could stay living there, and I just panicked. I even linked him with Madelaine McCann, since his second daughter had a similar eye defect to Madelaine's, which made me think maybe he had had something to do with that. I was spiralling up so fast I couldn't do anything about it, and my training with abused children made me think that at all costs I *must* express my worries about Jeremy; after all, he had been awful with me and my friends, and I thought it might still be going on. Even if I was wrong, I felt it was worth bringing him to the police's attention. He was duly interviewed and cautioned, and by that time I had been admitted to a mental health unit in Coventry, where I stayed for a month.

I have almost no memory of my time there. Charles tells me that I was a completely different person, sometimes obsessed with being able to touch my toes and making up little tests for him to try, such as telling him I had lost my glasses case and could not remember what it looked like. Once he had tried to remember, I produced it and said it had been a trick to see if he could describe it. But as I say, I have no recollection of any of that. Nigel got compassionate leave and came to see me every day. At first he took me home for the afternoon, but I got so upset by going back that he was advised not to do that, so we went for walks instead to a country park nearby to look at the birds.

CHAPTER 37

ALAN (NIGEL'S DAD)

Nigel was home for Christmas that year, and we had a celebration at our house for the whole family again. I had come out of hospital on 19 December, and we were just trying to keep things as normal as we could. Nigel's dad, Alan, was not with us on Christmas Day, as he had unexpectedly gone into hospital just before Christmas. We all visited him in hospital on Christmas Day, and he was in good spirits, opening his presents from everyone. On Boxing Day, Nigel's dad, Alan, died in hospital after a few days of being there with a heart problem. He was 93, and up until then had been in fairly good health, so although it was not really a surprise, it obviously affected us all, and my medication needed to be reviewed again. I had further time signed off work again, trying to get my drugs right, and Nigel was signed off sick too, as he was so stressed as well.

It was a difficult time and resulted in me almost resigning from my job, as I felt I could no longer cope with the stress. My consultant advised me, just in the nick of time, *not* to resign or make any other life-changing decisions whilst I was so unsettled. Nigel phoned my headmaster to explain that I was not resigning (as he seemed to think I should) but that I was now signed off sick until March. In the end, though, we decided that my health was more important than my salary, and I resigned that summer.

CHAPTER 38

JANE (NIGEL'S MUM)

It was useful that I wasn't going to work, as Nigel's mum, Jane, became very poorly shortly after that too. She had a car accident in the doctor's car park and decided to stop driving since the car was written off. Shortly after Alan's funeral and the scattering of his ashes, she was flooded out of her flat by a leak from upstairs. She had ordered a new kitchen for herself before that happened, and so she postponed that and stayed with various members of the family for a week at a time. She decided eventually to go into residential care for a while, while the flat was dried out and redecorated, and she had all new carpets and a new kitchen put in. It took a long time, and she was very stressed, of course. Her breathing became worryingly laboured, she had a leg infection that was not clearing up, and she wasn't coping very well at all.

In the end, Nigel's older brother decided to call an ambulance while he was with her, and she was taken into hospital. Between us, we visited every day. She said as soon as she was admitted that she wanted a do not resuscitate (DNR) order put in place. She never came out, dying on 28 November 2018. We had her funeral at the crematorium, as we had done with Alan, followed by a celebration of her life at our church, again the same as we did for Alan. It seemed fitting to scatter her ashes in the same spot too, and we arranged to do that on 7 June 2019—their wedding anniversary.

CHAPTER 39

WORKING FROM HOME

I had been working for Pets & People for years, on and off. When we had our own spaniel, I had been a carer for them, and so had had other dogs to stay when their owners were on holiday. It was a great scheme for me; I had another dog to look after along with my own, and the guest's food was provided, along with treats, bedding, poo bags, and a daily routine. I also got paid around £10 or £11 per day of the stay, so it was a win-win situation for me. Once I stopped working in schools, I thought of what I could do instead, and I decided to go back to Pets & People. I hadn't worked for them for about three years since our dog had died, but they still had me on their books and welcomed me back. It was lovely to have dogs around again!

At the same time, Nigel bought me a new sewing machine for my birthday, and I set about making bags using a pattern I had got in a magazine, and soon I had made lots of them. I opened an Etsy store online and started selling them, and I went to local craft fairs and sold at my stalls there too. I also learnt to crochet and made lots of flat animal bookmarks, which were very popular on my stalls. I started to make my own clothes, which went well too.

I was now, more than ever before, happy and fulfilled.

CHAPTER 40

RAINBOWS

I love rainbows; they mean so much to me. I feel that they are God's promise to us and are so breathtakingly beautiful. I once made up an acrostic for "RAINBOW" when I was feeling very high and excited about life:

Radiant,
Awesome,
Inspirational,
Nature's
Bow
Of
Wonder

To me the colours are significant:

Red = anger = stop
Orange = fiery, resentful = slow down and think.
Yellow = sunny-natured child = Charles's favourite colour!
Green = Go! Go! Go!
Blue = despair = colour of the sea
Indigo = inky depths
Violet = light at the end of a tunnel

Rainbows are certainly beautiful things, and you can imagine our surprise when on 16 March 2004 Charles and I saw one which was the wrong way up! We took photos and sent them to the meteorological weather society, who confirmed we were not seeing things and that it was, in fact, a circumzenithal arc we had seen. This is not actually a rainbow but a vividly coloured arc caused by the sunlight refracting off flat ice crystals in the atmosphere; it appears in the sky, not touching the horizon but floating free. It is a beautiful sight which we have seen since, now that we know what we are looking for. In fact, they appear just as often as normal rainbows but are not seen because they are directly overhead, and so many people go around looking at the ground. Our photograph, to our delight, was published in *The Cloud Book* by David & Charles in 2008.

I sometimes think of my list of rainbow colour meanings and then turn it up the other way, as if in a circumzenithal arc, so we go all the way back to red and to "stop". New life begins here.

CHAPTER 41

HINDSIGHT

As far as I can see, with that marvellous ability of having hindsight, I think that as a child I had, or was bordering on having, undiagnosed Tourette's syndrome (I don't know much about it, but what I do know I was displaying) starting when I was about 9 or 10. I still, even now, sometimes have to consciously squash the urge to kick, jerk, or gutturally cry "huh" out loud when I feel stressed. I was certainly displaying enough symptoms to, if I were doing it now as a child of that age in the present educational climate, also be considered to be somewhere on the autistic spectrum.

My treatment, as a young child and teenager taken away from home, was wrong and unforgivable, but it was all there was on offer at the time. I know the adults involved wanted to help me and did care, and I am still friends with, and keep in touch with the ones I valued the most. I do feel let down, but it was only because I was born too early to benefit from today's expertise with children like me. I now, as an adult, have the diagnosis of bipolar disorder (manic-depressive disorder). I now regularly take strong medication which works while I am asleep overnight but lets me enjoy life when I am awake.

My son, having begun to show difficulties at an early age, now has a diagnosis of Asperger's syndrome, which is an autistic spectrum disorder (ASD) umbrella term covering any strange behaviour, particularly social difficulties. He also suffers with dyslexia and dyspraxia. I said immediately, as soon as he began to show problems, that I wanted the difficulties to stop here.

My husband was confused at how strongly I felt; he didn't think it mattered too much and that Charles would be all right without getting outside help involved. But then, he didn't go through my experiences and couldn't understand how frightened I was.

I wanted to properly know exactly what was going on with Charles so we could help him quickly. I appreciate that he will never be "cured", any more than I will, but he is certainly outgrowing his difficulties as he gets older and matures.

He does not take any medication, even though I was offered Ritalin for him a few times.

He is now, at 24, an incredibly upbeat happy young man, the delight of me, his dad, and his employers, as he always tries so hard and is polite and caring. He doesn't make friends easily, but he does have two very good groups of friends, with whom he enjoys D&D (Dungeons and Dragons) role playing games. He is fully employed, loves his job, and rents a gorgeous little terraced house in our town, where he works. We see him at weekends.

Charles is a joy to me, and he understands about his difficulties and knows that they are genetic; that is, he understands that his own children may one day exhibit similar difficulties. But he is aware and ready to get help for them too, if necessary. The biggest outcome of all this is that I have discovered a patience I never knew I had with children like me and like Charles, to the extent that I trained for qualifications and became a special educational needs teaching assistant. I am constantly told that I am an authority on these matters, and that I am marvellously calm and caring towards these children. I have had such huge successes already with all of the children I have supported over the years.

It isn't exaggerating to say that I feel blessed to be able to understand and help these children. Whereas others are intimidated by their behaviours, these children seem to relate to me so well.

After Nigel's decision to have a vasectomy, I spent so many nights praying that I would somehow be given more children. I thought it was a selfish prayer and felt bad about praying it, but it kept popping into my prayers without me thinking about it, and now, with Annie, Andy, Rosie, Robert, Oscar, Trent, Daniel, Timmy, Jack, Sam, Ned, and all the other children on the SEN spectrum I have met at work, I feel that I have them after all. I am truly blessed.

Lightning Source UK Ltd.
Milton Keynes UK
UKHW011817081019
351238UK00001B/48/P